# THE SHATTERED HOUSE

## "Escape from Broken"

## Brittany Hall

# DEDICATION

I would like to dedicate this book to all the girls who were told they couldn't. My sister, you CAN, and you WILL.

# TABLE OF CONTENTS

# FOREWARD

It is a great honor to be asked to write the foreword to this book. The author, who just happens to be my oldest daughter, has been my rock through the last seven tumultuous years of my life. After being married for 25 years, my husband came home one day and announced he did not want to be married to me anymore. After some investigative work, I discovered the affair with someone he worked with. I was left devastated because I thought this man and I would certainly grow old together. Seven years after we separated, I am happier than I've ever been. I never realized how controlling this man was. It is so refreshing to be able to decide where to eat, to travel or to go shopping if I desire. For all those years, those decisions were his. If I did not go along with him, the repercussions were usually weeks of anger and silence on his part.

Unfortunately, my daughter married a man, who like her father, was extremely controlling. He did not want her out of his sight. She had to tell him her EVERY move. Even having dinner with me resulted in a phone call from him to check to see if she was really with me. Repercussions for her not doing exactly what he said usually resulted in her being thrown out of the house. Watching her go through everything she went through with him made me realize how strong she was. He had torn her down emotionally. By birth, she is my daughter. By choice, she is my best friend.

# ACKNOWLEDGMENTS

I would first like to thank my soulmate for pushing me to tell my story and for his continued support throughout the process. I would also like to thank my mom for being a pillar of strength for me no matter how hard life got. I am honored that I get to leave a piece of myself in the world. My hope is that by sharing my experiences, I can help at least one person survive or even avoid the misery of an abusive relationship.

# INTRODUCTION

F rom the outside in, we were your typical middle-class family. Looking through the lenses of most people's vantagepoint, we closely resembled the Huxtable family from the 90's sitcom "The Cosby Show." See, we were the ideal family above the surface. My parents were married, my mom was a tender age 19 and my dad was 26 when they got married. They were a pretty young couple to say the least. Dad excelled in the field of education and became a prominent teacher for the city in which we lived. Mom worked as a librarian, but also had the responsibility for the home. They didn't waste much time starting a family.

I seemed to have a happy life growing up compared to others I encountered or so I thought I did. At least my family dynamic was intact my young mind thought. Nights consisted of family dinners with parents and siblings. No phones were allowed at the table. For example, dinner was well-structured and organized. Without fail, we were all going to sit down each night and talk about our day. I can still picture the contentment on my face, the routine was reassuring, and I never once second guessed the "do as you're told" expectation in our household. At this point, I didn't really realize there was another option. I was still very naïve to the world and had not learned what I wanted. The feeling was more so to trust my parents because they knew best.

My parents' roles were very stereotypical or traditional in that my mom was the one who did all the cooking, all the cleaning, all the laundry, anything involved with kids, and my dad just made the money. Mom and Dad's relationship was built up like a happily ever after scene from a best-selling novel.

I didn't know it then, but my mother was very submissive, and Dad made all the decisions with little to no resistance. This was my first mental polaroid about the silhouette of what women were supposed to do. What I saw was a woman submitting to a man and just doing what he says, and that's how they raised us. Follow directions without question. Smile for the camera. It didn't matter what we saw as kids or what we all felt. It was ingrained in my head that children should be seen, not heard. You don't talk back, so I never could find my voice. For years, I felt like although I was steadily talking, I'd been placed on mute. If Mom and Dad said do it, that's just what I had to do. It didn't matter that I had a difference of opinion or whether I thought the opposite. When and whatever they said goes. My lips would move, but my voice was silent in decision making. I eventually stopped speaking up.

My dad had a relationship with my siblings and me vicariously through my mom. Although we were inside of the same house, we interacted with our father virtually. Yes, we were in the house together the whole time, but mom was the leader in making the connection between the kids and him. He really didn't do stuff with us. My mom was always the bridge that connected us to my dad. Dad never really tried. I don't remember much effort on his part to connect with us directly during my childhood. Of course, there are some good memories. Dad coming home in a good mood and wrestling with us, or the one time he went all out for Valentine's day for my sister and me. The big thing I remember was any time we'd eat dinner, he'd say to me and my sister, "Y'all going to help your mom clean up the kitchen?" I always thought, "Why can't you help? You sat and ate this meal just like we did. Why can't you clean up too?" These were just one of the many internal conversations I'd play tennis with inside my head but dared not to say them out loud.

As a nine-year-old girl, you can't say things like that because that's disrespectful. So, I chose to mind my manners. Hindsight is 20/20. I know that set me up for failure as far as seeing how relationships are structured. See, I became passive and imploded like some of you reading this page at this very moment. I relinquished my voice and replaced it with silent frustration(s).

The truth be told, I wasn't really surrounded by any other successful couples growing up. One aunt was married with children, but I didn't see their relationship, I just saw my cousins. The other aunt was a single mom and I wasn't given a backstage to see or observe her personal life. My mom's friends were single mothers. My dad's friends were all bachelors, so I didn't have any other image of a successful, or what I thought was a fruitful relationship other than them. I thought it worked. I thought what I saw modeled before me was the norm. Mom and Dad were the standard.

We lived in a house jammed packed with secrets buried deeply beneath our walls. Some of these secrets are as painful as the pen I'll let leak on to the pages of this book. If there was a problem, we simply ignored or painted over it to hide the blemishes because what happened in the house definitely stayed inside of our home. We had to 'protect the family.'

Growing up, I guess I was kind of in a relationship bubble. I was inexperienced in relationships, and I didn't date. The truth be told, I didn't start dating until age 17. I went out with someone who my family knew through playing tennis, so he was always with my family. Let's just say I played it safe. The next guy I dated in college. My parents detested him. Dad and Mom felt he had taken their homegrown princess down a dark road leading to nowhere. Although I respected their opinion, I still proceeded to see him. That was my bad boyfriend phase so that was hard. During this time, I was sneaking around to see him. I guess part of me was loving living life on the edge as a college student with an edgy boyfriend. Maybe this was a snapshot of me gaining or declaring my independence or the rush of the adventure. The closer my boyfriend and I became, the more my parents were determined to run interference. My parents hated him and pretty much shut the entire relationship down. I think that's why my dad stepped in later to be like, "This is the type of guy you should date." Remember it didn't matter what I wanted, what Daddy and Mommy said goes. Little did I know I was being groomed and set up for an imperfect handoff.

# CHAPTER 1

# THE HANDOFF

Ladies, have you longed for the day to be given away? Many looking at this page this very moment have spent their entire life planning for the perfect handoff to the perfect guy. Come on, let's be totally transparent. I was no different. As little girls we've all envisioned as we looked out into the mirrors of our future some time or another walking down the aisle on our wedding day looking flawless in our tailor-made wedding dress. Makeup and lashes flawless glistening from the rays of sunlight caressing our faces. The crowd standing at attention to the anthem to the beat of dun... dun... ta ...dun ... dun.. dun.. ta ...dun ...hand-in-hand with our father or father figures on the way to meet our Mr. Right at the altar. Excited about the process of wedding someone that at least our father and mother approved of. Now pause with me and take a deep breath in, then exhale slowly and imagine that perfect vision **shattered** by the harsh reality of the unexpected. Next, think about being hand-delivered to a familiar family face on purpose.

Since I have your attention, let's start at the very beginning. As I stated before, my dad was an educator in the public-school system in the town where I grew up. Dad was extremely proficient at his job and had a way with empowering young African American boys. During his tenure as a fourth-grade teacher, the school decided they were going to do gender-based classrooms. My dad, as a black male instructor, was assigned an inclusive male classroom because it was an inner-city school targeted to impacting all black males.

The school started a mentoring program for troubled kids because Malcolm was labeled as one of the problem children. The truth of the matter was Malcolm couldn't sit still to save his life. Malcolm spent most of the day flying paper airplanes through the building and turning classrooms upside down or inside out. Malcolm had a history of disruptive behaviors and had a target on his back labeled "problem child." Due to Malcolm's need for guidance, my dad took him under his wing through the fourth-grade mentoring program.

## THE FIRST SHOWING

I remember it like it was yesterday. The first time I laid my eyes on Malcolm. I wouldn't say we had any type of relationship then, but I remember my dad bringing him to the house. We were outside having a great time playing together like normal kids. Malcolm and I had a lot of fun that day running around the house. I can recall thinking to myself that Malcolm was not the troublemaker many made him out to be. Where was this monster that I heard second hand about? I was playing with him up close and couldn't find the bad boy anywhere. Maybe the label stuck on Malcolm was unwarranted or uncalled for. On the other hand, could it be that in all the hustle and bustle of playing that I overlooked something? Could it be that the monster growing within Malcolm was buried deep inside of the innocence of his youth? Only time will tell if time would reveal it to me at all.

The funny thing is we never really interacted much after that, but I would always recall him from our first encounter at my parent's house. If you show me a picture I could say, "Oh, yeah, I remember that," but there was no emotion there. Malcolm was in the fourth grade, he was nine, so I was five. Four or five, I guess? Not much memory there.

That was the first meeting, but definitely sure not our last. My dad and Malcolm continued to build their relationship throughout grade school and beyond. The two of them remained in constant contact throughout the years as my dad watched Malcolm's metamorphosis from a boy into a man. Dad was provided a backstage pass into Malcolm's developmental stages and was able to see him appear to do a 180-degree turn in his life. From my dad's perspective, Malcolm had shed the layers of skin (almost like a snake does) of his past and was well on his way to becoming a distinguished gentleman.

## THE SECOND SHOWING

See, my dad raved over the fact that Malcolm had left the local area and enlisted into the military. Dad reported that Malcolm had done very well for himself while in the military and I believe he felt proud since he had hands-on experience with mentoring and grooming him all those years. In my humble opinion, it seemed that Malcolm was the son that my dad never had, but the epitome of what he would want a son to be. Well, at least the son he would ascribe to have above the surface.

The next time I remember him coming around, I had just finished college. I'd just graduated, so it was 2010. I was still living at home with my parents and my dad was like, "Come ride with me. I'm going to meet an old student for lunch." Okay, so we all piled in a car and we're on our way to meet someone at Wendy's not too far from my house. Remember what Daddy said went. I had no clue or couldn't guess who we're going to meet since he had taught so many students in the past. This random turn of events would change my life. Pulling up in the parking lot of Wendy's, I remember thinking who we were going to see at the spur of the moment. It wasn't a surprise that Daddy would drag us all along from time to time, but I sensed a level of excitement in his demeanor. I felt a faint strangeness in the air that I couldn't quite place into words. This could've been because I was over *shattered* by my suspense a little.

My father jumped out of the car and began leading the way through the door of Wendy's with the rest of my family following. Pause for a couple of seconds to take a wild guess to who I saw standing there. It was Malcolm. Not the boy version, but the grown up and mature Malcolm. I was cool with it because I had no feeling at that moment, only jaded memories of playing around the house. I was completely numb. So, he said hi. I said hello and digressed to becoming a spectator.

During lunch, Dad and Malcolm were catching up and everything. Malcolm had just gotten back from flight school because he was in Alabama getting his pilot's license to fly helicopters. It was the first time they had sat down and talked in a couple years, so they were reminiscing about old times. It was both ironic and fascinating that Malcolm went from flying paper planes, destroying classrooms, and exhibiting disruptive behaviors to defending and potentially piloting aircrafts for the United States of America. I must admit Malcolm's transformation really impressed me.

It was good listening to Malcolm and my dad's conversation on the sideline. It was borderline entertaining until out of nowhere, Dad put me in the game. My dad (smiling slightly) just threw in that, "Hey, you know my daughter's really sociable here. She is a socialite. Malcolm, since you're back in town, you probably don't have many friends. Y'all should hang out." Hold on, stop the press! Did my dad just set me up? Daddy, did you just give me a way to

Malcolm? Wait just one minute here! Did my father just hand me off like a quarterback hands a football to his star player to score a game-winning touchdown? Was it football? Was I being passed off? These were just some of the questions running through my head while everything around me seemed to be already played and planned out.

See, my dad was really pushy about it. At that time, I really respected my dad's opinion, so he was like, "You should hang out with Malcolm." Oh, he thinks Malcolm is a good person, maybe I should hang out with him. Inside I felt that my dad was looking out for my best interest since the guy I'd chosen to be with in college wasn't up to his and Mom's standards. Every girl hopes their dad protects them. I was no different from most daughters.

Malcolm was in agreement with Dad as they appeared to be team players and consenting that he and I go out. Afterall, Malcolm didn't have to ask me out, my dad had already opened the door, given him his blessing, and basically hand-delivered me. Before I knew it, a date was being set for the following night as my voice was still on mute. I simply went with the flow.

We went to the movies to see "The A- Team." The date went well and there is not too much you can mess up at the theater. We both were like, this is fun, let's go grab some drinks. So, we went out on Granby Street and I was a busybody as well as very outgoing back then. I knew all the bartenders in the city and truly enjoyed the night life. With that said, I was in a great position to paint the town red or whatever color I wanted. We went out, had a great time, got intoxicated as we raised our *unshattered* glasses under the night sky. Afterwards, mixing laughs with drinks, we came back to the house still under the influence. Throughout the remainder of the night, we flirted off and on, but did not sleep together the first night, but after that, we were pretty much together all the time.

Malcolm and I seemed to have reconnected at the ideal time because I wasn't dating anyone else. I had just gotten out of college and I was working as a waitress. I would work at night and get up around 1:00 or 2:00 pm the next day. Malcolm would be getting off work around the time I was waking up, so he would come over and we'd hang out after that through the evening and the night. My relationship with Malcolm was extremely exciting. Malcolm was tall, light skinned, muscular, handsome, charming, and extremely attentive to me. It was as if he was studying me and anticipated my every need by placing an emphasis on every detail that concerned me. This was one thing I really remember standing out to me. I had a Ford Explorer Sport Truck and the battery died. I was left stranded trying to get to work or something, and so Malcolm pretty much just took care of me. He came to pick me up and we battery boosted the car. Then Malcolm took me to shop to secure a battery replacement. He paid for the battery. Malcolm just took care of it, so I guess that gave me a sense of feeling protected and valued because of him going out of his way in order to make sure I was okay. Malcolm didn't have to buy me a car battery. This was my car, not his. Yet, Malcolm took my matter into his own hands and handled it. I remember that sticking out to me. That was really early in our relationship. May or June after we met.

Malcolm was a very strong personality. Malcolm had a brilliant mind. He was very smart and savvy. Malcolm was really good at owning situations and loved to lead. If we walked into a room, he had to be the center of attention. If not, he would command it one way or another. Malcolm's desire to be the focal point was fine for me, though, because I don't like being the center of attention, so he would take that pressure away from me which, at the time, I thought was cool.

He would speak up for me. He was the type of man to order for me at dinner. Malcolm would order my drink. He didn't know what I was in the mood for, but here's your drink. Malcolm didn't ask; he simply did what he felt was right for me. Malcolm was five years older than me. I was so young and coming from a household where I felt I did what I was supposed to do, and that is one of my biggest regrets. I never did what I wanted to do; I did what I was supposed to do.

In addition, despite the fact that Malcolm and I didn't see each other a lot until we began to date, there were so many parallels and intersections where our lives intertwined. For example, Malcolm's aunt was also in the school system and his uncle was a mentor to my dad. There was this family history, so there were lots of things to talk about. The more I thought about it, we overlapped in so many ways. We didn't have a similar background growing up, but the intermittent mingling of the family gave us a launch point.

Malcolm was very exciting and totally fun to be around. Malcolm possessed a charismatic energy that lured me into the confines of his space. He was available. He had time to spend. He had just gotten back from flight school, so he had money to spend. We were always going somewhere, doing something. Going out doing things mattered to me a lot at that time. The money was nice, you know? It's cool to be able to do fun things versus the college kids I had been dating where going to Sonic was a hot date.

This was the perfect combination for me as I was seeking to establish myself in all the areas of my life being fresh out of college. My relationship with Malcolm was happening fast and if I could choose a setting to define it, it would be turbo. If our relationship was a car, it would've been a top of the line Ferrari with more than the capacity to ignore all of the warning signs and break all of the speed limits.

Although the relationship was moving full speed ahead, it took me a very long time to get to that point of being in love with Malcolm. Truly it wasn't a story of love at first sight for a number of reasons. The guy I dated in college, I guess I was still hung up on him at the time. I'd moved on physically, but still stuck in emotions of my past relationship. I was still imprinted by the pain that my previous relationship had caused. I was definitely hesitant to allow myself to feel. Pain is something I did my best to shy away from. That's just how I am. I'm not a lead with my heart person at all. It was just hanging out. It was fun, it was simple.

In hindsight, I don't think I was ready to settle down, but I couldn't date anyone else. At the time, it was like a bright light was over me that blinded my view from anyone else. Malcolm was my blind spot. Have you ever tried to look out into the distance on a sunny day without filters? I'm certain you have encountered that light piercing your vision as you fumbled through your belongings in search for shades. The light of this new and unexpected relationship blinded me from any other options.

I couldn't see anything else, but it didn't even matter. I don't think I choose to, it just happened. I was in this relationship by handoff. There was no aha moment. It was just, I met him, we dated strongly the whole summer, and by the fall, we're in a relationship. So, if my relationship with Malcolm was a car (Ferrari), I was just hanging out for the fast ride in the beginning.

To say my parents were accepting of Malcolm would be an understatement. It was, hey, we're going on a family vacation, can Malcolm come? Malcolm was considered family by second nature and was always invited. If my family was going anywhere or doing anything, the question that immediately asked would be if Malcolm could come. Having the acceptance of my parents set the tone for Malcolm and our relationship. It was easy in that regard; it wasn't like I was dating the bad boy and had to sneak around to see him and stuff like that. Malcolm was just as part of my family as I was.

Besides, my dad and mom approved it and officially handed me over to Malcolm. Well, what else was I supposed to do? My dad thought he was a good match, and I'm certain that's why I overlooked a lot of the things in the process of being passed to Malcolm.

# REFLECTIONS

**(Feel free to journal your thoughts and learning experiences by answering the questions below).**

HOW DID YOU FEEL WHEN READING THIS CHAPTER?

_____

_____

_____

_____

_____

WHAT DID YOU LEARN?

_____

_____

_____

_____

_____

HOW CAN YOU USE THIS INFORMATION TO HELP SOMEONE ELSE IN LIFE?

_____

_____

_____

_____

_____


HOW DOES THE CONTENT OF THIS CHAPTER RELATE TO YOUR LIFE EXPERIENCE(S)?

_____

_____

_____

_____

_____

# CHAPTER 2

# BUILDING

The most important component to building any sustainable structure is securing a stable foundation. It doesn't really matter how beautiful the exterior of a house is, if the foundation isn't fortified, it will ultimately crumble. In other words, what's built or erected isn't as nearly important as what it's established on. Picture standing inside of your dream home with everything you desire on the outside and inside. The decor within the home is just like you always wanted it to be only to discover that the house you built your foundation on is wobbly, unsound, uncertain, compromised, and *shattered* groundwork. Once the conditions of the foundation are revealed, one of two things will happen. Either the value of the home instantly depreciates or surges. No matter how dainty or lovely the exterior of the house, the base will always speak truth.

The same is true in relationship-building. Every association is a byproduct of the foundation it was created upon. My relationship wasn't any different.

Malcolm and I started forming our relationship on a foundation of what we assumed each other to be. The two of us had so many parallels and intersections.

We were constructing our relationship as we went along based on an idea that it could work because of our familiar connections. It was especially risky that Malcolm and I established a bond based on third party influence. In doing so, I overlooked the roots growing deep underneath the surface of our relationship.

## ROOTS IN THE FOUNDATION

These roots stemming from our past provided for bumpy footing in our relationship. Remember when I said I lived in a house of family secrets? So did Malcolm. Our two worlds collided like a pair of wine glasses meeting at the conclusion of a toast and before we knew it, both the unknown and what we thought we comprehended were now spewing over and pouring into each other.

Malcolm was the oldest of three boys. His middle brother was 'the one who never moved out,' and his younger brother did okay, but he was younger than me. At the time, I think he was finishing up college and he had joined the Army. They weren't close at that time for whatever reasons.

Malcolm's mom was a drug addict and wrestled with the vices of addiction their entire childhood. He and his siblings were void of their mother's love during all of their developmental years. I firmly believe that the abandonment Malcolm and his brothers suffered directly impacted them. Malcolm's uncle, the one who helped raise him was a mentor to my father. That's who raised them because his mom was struggling on and off with drugs. As you can see, even Malcolm's family was intermingled with mine beyond his and my dad's connection. Mine and Malcolm's roots were running deep underneath the surface.

Malcolm's dad was unmannerly, physically abusive towards his mom. His family fled from Chicago when he was a baby to escape from him in hopes of obtaining a better life. Years later his dad passed away before they ever had a chance to fix their relationship.

I know for a fact that *shattered* Malcolm.

Malcolm talked to me about all the pain his dad caused him and his family while we were assembling our bond. Malcolm went on to share with me that he resented his father's abusive and destructive behaviors and how he didn't want to be that way. He spoke of the harsh memories of his parents fighting, and his dad hitting his mom. We had in-depth conversations about how he never wanted to be like his dad. Malcolm vowed to take a different course in life and not replay his father's mistakes.

By the time I reconnected with Malcolm, his mom wasn't on drugs anymore. She had been clean and sober for several years. Malcolm's mom was living a normal life, working a minimum wage job, and cohabitating with her boyfriend in a two-bedroom apartment. It was her, the man she was dating, and Malcolm's little brother because he's never left home. Malcolm was sleeping on the floor at her apartment. His mom had come a long way from where she was many years before. Due to my value on family, I was so happy to hear that despite not being with Malcolm throughout the journey.

Nevertheless, I could clearly see Malcolm's generational curses or challenges like nails protruding from broken boards in the floor. It is obvious, but yet so unclear. We kept right on walking it out with the occasional prick of discomfort.

On the other hand, I had no room to judge Malcolm since I had my own roots to deal with. Listen, my roots had been buried and sworn to the secrecy of my family for years. Think about when I said there were three of us growing up together in my household. Well, I didn't tell you about my fourth sibling yet.

Okay, let's recap. I was the oldest, then there was my sister and my little brother. My dad had another daughter older than me, but I didn't even know she existed until I was almost 15 or 16. Imagine the shock to be moved from the first to the middle. We weren't even allowed to talk about the indiscretion or say her name above a whisper. Everything in the household was about perception. The house was to look good on the outside even if the inside had gaping holes in the structure. My brother and sisters and I were constantly reminded by my dad not to let the secret leak out. Even now I can still hear his voice ring in the hallways of my mind saying, "Don't let anyone know I got this child out of wedlock and don't talk about her outside of the family. I know you're upset right now, but we've got to go to this event so smile." It was completely about perception. I didn't know that we were hiding the dysfunction. This was a bitter pill for a sixteen-year-old girl to swallow.

At the time, I didn't know. I had no clue. I had a very happy, blessed childhood, and I never wanted for anything. There were some good morals instilled. There were some bad characteristics I picked up, but I know it wasn't intentional. It was just that was the best they could do. They didn't really know any better. Again, my mom was 19 when they got married. In hindsight, it seemed as if Mom, Dad, and my siblings all grew up together.

If you believe in growing pains, you can identify with the fact that my family had more than their share.

In my house, having a good education was embedded into the center of our moral fabric. Pursuing a good education was not an option. If education was a sermon, it was preached to my siblings and me more than just on Sundays. All I was trained to do was go to high school and make good grades so that I could get into college. I ended up securing a full ride scholarship to college, played sports, and graduated cum laude. The bar had been raised (by my parents) and I leaped and scaled over them. The next thing I was supposed to do was find a husband and get married. Yes, you read it correctly. I was to discover a man and get wedded. After all, I was expected to follow in the roots of my family tree. Academics, graduation, and marriage were instilled (in that order) or deeply rooted in my upbringing.

## BROKEN TOOLS

Now that I've uncovered a part of our origins, it's imperative to note that we would only be able to use what we had been given to build rapport in this relationship. We had issues to work through stemming from the seeds that were dropped into the soil of our lives. Though these matters were lingering quietly under the subfloor of our union, they were destined to emerge.

Regardless of everything we saw in ourselves given the fragments of history he and I exchanged with each other, we kept on building with broken tools. Again, I say we could only use the instruments, devices, and means afforded to us by the generation before us. Looking back, I can say we didn't even know how to build yet. We were diving headfirst into our own construction site.

Malcolm and I didn't even know how to form a healthy relationship, nevertheless, we were now in an unhealthy one. He had never seen a healthy relationship directly and although I thought I had, it couldn't have been any further from the truth. Nonetheless, we were still determined for whatever reason to assemble this relationship without reading any of our warning labels and personalized instructions. Malcolm and I simply whipped out our *shattered* tools that we'd collected from the broken box our lives were contained in and went to work on each other rather than ourselves. Can you identify with trying to fix external things in someone else before you repair internal ones? Malcolm and I were just doing what we had been taught in life class. Understand that we were building upon the backs of our own brokenness. Malcolm and I were hemorrhaging, but still hammering away. Malcolm and I were broken, however, pulling on each other. We were determined to screw in the nuts of our past and fill in the holes of the dry walls of our earlier years. He and I had no idea what we were building with the remnants of ***shattered*** tools, but we kept on constructing.

# REFLECTIONS

**(Feel free to journal your thoughts and learning experiences by answering the questions below).**

HOW DID YOU FEEL WHEN READING THIS CHAPTER?

_____

_____

_____

_____

_____

WHAT DID YOU LEARN?

_____

_____

_____

_____

_____

HOW CAN YOU USE THIS INFORMATION TO HELP SOMEONE ELSE IN LIFE?

_____

_____

_____

_____

_____

HOW DOES THE CONTENT OF THIS CHAPTER RELATE TO YOUR LIFE EXPERIENCE(S)?

_____

_____

_____

_____

_____

# CHAPTER 3

❧

# Dirty Windows

## IN YOUR WINDOWS

**W***indows,* in my opinion, are one of the most overlooked features of home. Often windows aren't the first thing individuals look at when viewing a house for the first time. With so many other dimensions of a house that demand attention, it's easy to overlook the ***windows*** until they need to be cleaned. When the windows are damaged, they become an eyesore. Even the smallest speck of dirt can be noticed when it's time to look out to the world from inside. If eyes are the ***windows*** to the soul, I was starting to see Malcolm's a little clearer through the ***shattered*** glass.

Now that Malcolm and I were exclusive, the mask was coming off. I started to see things unravel in Malcolm that still gives me chills today. Slowly, I noticed that nothing I did truly was good enough for him. The more I fed into attempting to fulfill Malcolm's needs, the more depleted I felt within as a woman. There was nothing more painful than to be asked to be a participant in a relationship where you don't have a pot to piss in or a ***window*** to throw it out of. Truly, I wasn't afforded the common courtesy to have equal say in the relationship. In other words, Malcolm was taxing or demanding withdrawals from our relationship account without being willing to make the proper investment(s).

Malcolm was always stuck in 'I' instead of 'we' mode. It was always my fault when a disagreement or an argument would arise.

Pouring out so much energy daily was slowly taking its toll on my emotional state. I began to feel that I was trapped inside a mental chess match as I struggled to anticipate Malcolm's next move. Even when I thought I knew the rules of engagement, Malcolm would change, invert the rules of the relationship, and shift the board.

Malcolm had a way with words. He used to say things like, "This relationship is really serious for me, I don't want to play games. I'm at a point in my life where I'm ready to be settled down." It was as if Malcolm, more frequently than not, was giving me a disclaimer or ultimatum. Daily I was consistently reminded of his agenda of settling down. It was almost like we were already on a timer. Unbeknownst to me, Malcolm had already placed us in his window of time. Malcolm was ready to settle down and to him that's all that mattered. I was rarely asked how I felt about our relationship and if so, I wasn't heard through the shade of all the dirt in the *windows* from Malcolm.

No matter the tone, Malcolm's words sounded like battleship sirens in my ears and heart. I always kept my guards up because I was never aware when the blunt of his words would strike me.

I felt obligated to fit into the mold of what he needed, and that would set the tone for the entire relationship. I was constantly trying to do my best to fit into Malcolm's oversized demands. So many questions and cross examinations. Do you still have feelings for any of your ex's? Are you talking to anyone else? Do you find anyone from your past attractive? Are you sure that you really want to be with me? Being asked by Malcolm some of the following questions repeatedly drove me up the wall and at times made me want to jump out of the *window* at times.

When I didn't give Malcolm the response he wanted or thought he needed, all verbal hell would begin to break loose. Instead of letting up when I retreated, Malcolm would bear down and use this *window* of opportunity to ask even more questions or rehash the ones he'd ask before. Malcolm didn't care how many times he'd asked the question, he was determined to get the answer he wanted whether it was the truth or not.

## THROWING DIRT

My sister and I are very close and have a strong bond. Once there was a time where my sister came over to the house to attend a cookout. I can recall everything being chill at first. She and I were having our normal girl talk about memories from the past, our love life, and men in general. From the conversation, we began scrolling through social media from her phone and stumbled up on a page from a past acquaintance. My sister and I began to comment back and forth about the gentleman's page. There wasn't anything disrespectful or derogatory, we were simply engaging in our conversation. Little did I know that Malcolm was eavesdropping and overheard the entire conversation and of course interrupted in his own way.

Malcolm became extremely livid in a way I had never seen him before. Malcolm was so irate that he couldn't contain himself almost like a pot that had been simmering on high for hours that was now reaching the boiling point. He immediately began to throw *dirt* my way. Malcolm started to tirade me with a bunch of questions right in front of my sister as if to show me no regard. Who are you guys talking about on social media? Whose photos are you liking? Why are you both disrespecting me? The questions went on and on like a broken record stuck on repeat. I was so embarrassed and if the floors could have opened and swallowed me up, I would have gladly obliged. This was the first time I felt dirty in our relationship. At that moment, I felt innocently guilty of something I didn't do. Again, I had been put on defense having to prove the intent of my actions to a jury of one.

I'd been faithful to Malcolm and wasn't interested in anyone else, yet he sought to paint me dirty or out to be a woman I was not. No woman should have to be put in a position to look out or be viewed from a stained *window* by the very person who claims they love you.

Malcolm was still enraged and wasn't done yet and insisted that my sister and everyone else leave the house immediately. Once everyone left the house, Malcolm reached up and pounded the glass chandelier above him knocking it down to the ground. *Shattered* pieces fell from the ceiling all over the floor beneath us.

Despite me explaining that we were just reminiscing and catching up, Malcolm still demanded that they exit. From that day forward, Malcolm tried his best to separate me from my sister and began to blame her for our relationship issues. Malcolm was, in my opinion, unwavering in keeping me at arms-length. If I wanted to go out with friends and family alone, an argument would emerge as he desired to keep me at *window* view.

In recollection, there was the time when I went to homecoming at the college I matriculated from. Malcolm was totally opposed to me going, but in that moment, something deep inside me said I'm going. See, I was missing my friends and college classmates and wanted to stay up to date with them. Needless to say, Malcolm was angry, and it had gotten to the point where I already anticipated it. Struggling with a mixture of fear and determination, I wouldn't relent this time. I recall my whole body cringing before going out for the evening, but I went anyway. You know that overwhelming and all-encompassing feeling that starts in the pit of your stomach, radiates through your chest and subsides in your throat? At homecoming I reminisced about all the fun I had during my college years. Surrounding myself with friends and associates was like someone had suddenly opened the *window* for those brief moments letting a breath of fresh air in and for a few hours I felt like myself. If I could describe my feelings at that time in two words, it would be free and feminine. All those good feelings I had would come to a screeching halt the instant I returned back to Malcolm and I knew it.

Returning home was going to be the worst part as I played a game of mental tennis in mind serving up my rebuttals to common questions Malcolm would ask. My intuition and my history as a star athlete prepared me for the match as I felt like the relationship from Malcolm's view had turned into a competition. I'd be ready. After all, I had done nothing wrong that would warrant an investigation, so I prepared to go on the offense and prepared my mental serve. Game on, I said in my mind as I turned the key to enter the place where we lived. Of course, Malcolm was upset with me and displayed the silent treatment at first, then the accusations and questions soon ensued.

Most of the time, I surrendered and declined an invite from friends and family regardless of how bad I wanted to accept the invitation of going out alone. I know now that wasn't the right thing to do the majority of the time, but I thought sacrificing for the relationship was the right thing to do. Nonetheless, the arguments with Malcolm increased the more I tried to decrease my feelings, dreams, and desires. Eventually, I could no longer see myself in this relationship. All I saw were filthy *windows*. All I could see from inside my point of view was a lopsided bond. I was constantly receiving the shorter end of the stick. This relationship was becoming an eyesore. The ***windows*** of the relationship were ***shattered*** and hanging off the hinges of emotional trauma.

# REFLECTIONS

**(Feel free to journal your thoughts and learning experiences by answering the questions below).**

HOW DID YOU FEEL WHEN READING THIS CHAPTER?

_____

_____

_____

_____

_____

WHAT DID YOU LEARN?

_____

_____

_____

_____

_____

HOW CAN YOU USE THIS INFORMATION TO HELP SOMEONE ELSE IN LIFE?

_____

_____

_____

_____

_____


HOW DOES THE CONTENT OF THIS CHAPTER RELATE TO YOUR LIFE EXPERIENCE(S)?

_____

_____

_____

_____

_____

# CHAPTER 4

⊘

# THE ACCIDENT

In life there are always the unexpected change(s) of events that even on your best day you couldn't change. The road we travel on the journey of life is bound to have twists and winding turns, hills and valleys. You know those pivotal moments where time appears to stand still while all of the air feels like it gets sucked out of the room(s) of your life and changes it completely? Have you ever received news that you always feared you'd hear, but yet and still you found yourself unprepared, unguarded and unraveled? On another note, take a few brief seconds to look back at a time when you fell, or something obstructed your movement unexpectedly. Do you remember the pain it caused? You may still bear the physical, emotional, and mental scars.

Can you call to mind a time where you or someone you loved had an *accident* of any kind? How did you feel within that moment? Where were you when you received the news? What impact did the *accident* have on your life? As I provide you with a deeper dive into my real-life accounts over the next couple of pages, I want you as the reader to keep these questions in mind.

## CRASH

It seems like a day ago, although it's been over a decade since the crash. I can remember that there was a lot of tension in the air already for a number of reasons. There was so much happening all around me ranging from family to personal issues. Honestly speaking, it appeared that my environment at the time was setting up a scene that would plot out a natural disaster in my life.

First off, it was my mom's birthday, February 25th. There was already tension because my dad had started having his affair. Mom was upset because dad left and wasn't home that weekend for her birthday. My dad had never missed her birthday and his absence and marital indiscretions totally devastated my mom and I was doing my absolute best to console her. At the same time, my heart was breaking and full to the brim with mixed emotions. I'd always looked up to dad and now a wedge had been forged in our relationship and respect had been lost. See, my ideal textbook family dynamic had just collided with the reality of the current dysfunction(s) my dad was betraying. I remember that space in time all too well. It was like two troubled oceans *crashing* together without pause.

As awful as this day was turning out to be, it was far from being over. Malcolm and I were stuck in our normal routine of arguing. I'm totally keeping it real when I say I can't think of what he and I were disputing. If I had to guess what he and I were feuding about, it was probably about me still allegedly having feelings for an ex. He was always hung up on that. It was always someone else, it was always cheating, it was always something or someone. Malcolm would always say, "You're not really committed to me because of him." That's probably what it was if I had to make an educated guess. Because of everything transpiring with my mom and dad, it seemed like everything was running together. What I do know for a fact is there was a heated exchange between Malcolm and I the previous night. I think he fell asleep on the couch the night before. Malcolm ended up staying overnight. He stayed overnight, but he got up earlier to leave because he wasn't supposed to be there due to the fact that I was still living with my parents. Staying overnight at my parent's house was a no no!

On the morning of February 25, 2011, Malcolm left my parent's home in a hurry and with a heavy heart. As Malcolm was leaving my parent's home early in the morning, he was involved in a terrible motorcycle *accident*.

The road was damp and slick from the morning dew. It was wintertime in February. It was cold that night before, and by morning it had started warming up a little causing the streets to be glassy.

Malcolm was making a right turn out of the neighborhood. The back tire of his motorcycle hit the line on the street and went out from under him. That's why he slid off his bike.

The house was actually on the corner, so I heard it. I'll never get the sound of the screeching tires and noise from the crash out of my memory. My bedroom was situated at the back of the house where the intersection was, so I heard the wheel vroom, then he called me and was like, "I got in an *accident*." My mom and I rushed to the scene and he was lying in the street. Luckily someone pulled over to assist Malcolm so he wasn't alone. He wasn't in pain at that point which was weird. I think he was in shock because he was talking to me like normal.

As I looked down to take a look closer, both of Malcolm's ankles were torn up. He had a road rash from where he had slid several feet. He didn't really hurt his body. It was just the way his bike fell. His ankles were in shambles. The force and momentum of the *crash* pushed Malcolm's ankles outward.

## The After Effects

Malcolm's accident occurred between six or seven in the morning. The ambulance arrives at the place of the tragedy. They check Malcolm's vitals and everything. Then the emergency medical technicians strapped Malcolm down and loaded him onto the stretcher. Next we went to the hospital and my mom was like, "You have to go to the hospital because when someone's in the hospital, you have to be there in case something happens." Despite the trauma my mom was experiencing in her life, she still remained full of compassion. "Okay," I replied. Not that I wanted to be at the hospital waiting room sitting and waiting all day, but my mom said that's what you're supposed to do when people go to the emergency room.

Mom and I sat there all morning. It was nearly afternoon by the time the doctors and nurses let me back to see him. Malcolm was really out of it. The medical team said they we're going to have to do surgery because they thought his ankle had been dislocated. The doctors explained that they were going to do an open reduction procedure to pop Malcolm's ankle back in place. At the time, we didn't even know about the right ankle. They just did X-rays on the left because they could see it was *shattered*.

Later on, the medical team administered X-rays on the right ankle, but it didn't show the tendons, so they didn't know what to say about that. They conducted the surgery, but they couldn't fix it. At this point we were all baffled including the surgeons. They're like, "We're going to have to refer him to a specialist." The end result of the *accident* had *shattered* Malcolm's left ankle and tore his Achilles in the right.

Looking back, I know this was the moment everything changed. In hindsight, there was truly no way we would be the same after this type of calamity.

Note Malcolm was rushed to the hospital for immediate surgery due to injuries on both ankles. My mom and I spent the day in the waiting room only to find out that the doctors were unable to treat his injuries due to their severity. We took him home with several future doctor's appointments on the calendar.

He was living with his mom at the time because he had just moved back to the area from pilot school and he was trying to find a house.

Malcolm didn't have an apartment or anything, he was just staying on a mattress at his mom's apartment until everything was finalized with the home he was purchasing. With very limited mobility, sleeping on a mattress was entirely out of the question and his mom's place was on the second floor of a building with no elevator. Malcolm was unable to walk for MONTHS so my parents offered to rent out the first-floor guest bedroom for him since his home was not wheelchair accessible. Malcolm accepted the offer from my parents, and we moved him in.

I singlehandedly took on his care. I was literally like a nurse to Malcolm. Isn't that what a woman is supposed to do for her man? I administered Malcolm's medications every four hours, gave daily sponge baths, took him to doctor's appointments, multiple surgeries, and physical therapy sessions. Yes, I took care of it all. I was there for Malcolm's beck and call. Malcolm became my life and daily responsibility.

After all of the care I provided Malcolm, one would think he would be extremely grateful. You would have thought that after going through the incident surrounding the *accident,* it would have humbled Malcolm, but he seemed to be numb by the *side effects*.

Malcolm's response to my care and support was mean. Daily I was met with anger in the face of me caring for him. Malcolm blamed me for the accident because of the disagreement the night before. He claims the accident happened because he was distracted by our argument and his head wasn't clear enough to be out riding. Another RED FLAG. Now I was being held responsible for his *accident.* At the time, all I wanted was for him to get better, so I made him my priority, and he took full advantage of it. It's crazy how displacement from someone can make you feel guilty for something you had no control over. Malcolm had a manipulative way of making me feel guilty by default. Truly, I had no influence on the *accident* or the outcome. I knew I wasn't accountable for the damage that had occurred, but Malcolm saw it differently. Slowly, I became Malcolm's verbal punching bag.

## LONG RECOVERY

I started my master's program in the fall of 2011 concurrent with my new responsibilities as a caregiver to my handicapped boyfriend (note the sarcasm). Still serving as Malcolm's primary caregiver, I was also taking classes at a nearby campus. This was the first time I was not at his beck and call since the *accident.* Me not being there 24/7 and doing something for me made Malcolm uneasy and he didn't hesitate to selfishly express that. I think that was the first time I saw him get mean. Whatever I did wasn't fast enough for Malcolm. He would say, "You're twenty minutes late on my medicine. You know I'm in pain." I'd say, "Well, take the pills." Absolutely everything started to become my fault.

The relationship became even more unbalanced. Malcolm was becoming more of a burden. He was unable to do anything on his own and had no issues relying on me for everything. After the accident, he couldn't do anything. He couldn't bathe, he couldn't go get food. Malcolm couldn't get up to go to the bathroom, so I was emptying urinals frequently. It was a lot.

Some would say I spoiled him rotten and I would have to agree with it. I was exhausted but felt a sense of ownership to him, so I kept giving. Even on empty I kept giving out.

During Malcolm's recovery process, he was also completing the purchase of his first house which realistically meant that I did all the onsite visits, meetings, and acted as a courier service for paperwork. In May of that year, he closed on the new house. I oversaw and facilitated all the work being done prior to moving in. Now I felt like I was serving as a real estate advisor slash personal assistant. Day in and day out, I was consistently under stress. Caring for Malcolm was a full-time job plus overtime. Fulfilling multiple roles in the relationship, I didn't feel like Malcolm's girlfriend at all because I was too busy serving in other capacities. Occupied with selecting flooring, paint colors, moving arrangements…while he criticized. By the summer, he had moved in and I was there by his side as he was STILL on bedrest and unable to walk or care for himself fully. Malcolm was constantly in pain, the injury was inoperable, and he was quickly becoming meaner and bitter by the day. Malcolm has lost more than just his mobility or his motorcycle on the wet pavement that winter morning. I believe he left a piece of himself there. Pieces of our relationship were left scattered on the roadside that day. See it was more than just Malcolm's *shattered* ankles as a result of an accident, it was far deeper than the turn of events itself. The *crash* was beginning to be symbolic of our two worlds colliding and the sum total of the damage our relationship was causing.

The full *recovery* I was hoping for Malcolm seemed more distant as time progressed. It was no way that Malcolm would ever fully *recover* and sad to say neither would I. Not to make light of the horrible accident that Malcolm endured, I feel like a huge part of me was left *shattered* from the **crash.**

# REFLECTIONS

**(Feel free to journal your thoughts and learning experiences by answering the questions below).**

HOW DID YOU FEEL WHEN READING THIS CHAPTER?

_____

_____

_____

_____

_____

WHAT DID YOU LEARN?

_____

_____

_____

_____

_____

HOW CAN YOU USE THIS INFORMATION TO HELP SOMEONE ELSE IN LIFE?

_____

_____

_____

_____

_____

HOW DOES THE CONTENT OF THIS CHAPTER RELATE TO YOUR LIFE EXPERIENCE(S)?

_____

_____

_____

_____

_____

# CHAPTER 5

# HANDS ON

According to the statistics provided by the National Domestic Violence Hotline, one in four women (24.3%) and one in seven men (13.8%) aged 18 and older in the United States have been the victim of severe physical violence by an intimate partner in their lifetime. Intimate Partner Violence (IPV) alone affects more than 12 million people across the U. S. each year. This is a serious problem but often preventable.

The power of human touch is truly a force to be reckoned with. Even the softest of touches leave an imprint of lifelong memories. When touch is used correctly, it can be used to soothe the soul, but utilized incorrectly it ignites a raging storm. Isn't it ironic the same hands that can hold and caress you can also be used to break, destroy or dismember you? Often it's hard to fathom that you can give yourself to people that don't even value who you are, and you're left taking the hit.

**THE AFFAIR**

Almost a year after the accident, the burdens of our relationship became too much for me and I sought solace in the arms of another man. It was subtle at first and then it got totally out of hand. Looking backwards, I can clearly tell that rejection, brokenness, and being unshielded led me to become unfaithful. During this time, I was so vulnerable because of the wear and tear of my relationship with Malcolm. I needed a safe place to land and ended up in an entanglement. Although the severity of what Malcolm and I were going through didn't give me a license to cheat, it left the door wide open for me to indulge in an affair. A mistake on my part, but part of the story, nonetheless. Besides, I was aware of what I was doing and owned it.

The affair – true story…the guy actually worked for my dad. My dad had introduced me to him a few years before as well. We'll call him Kris. It was another setup attempt but at that time he and I were only interested in sex. The entire situation was a 'friends with benefits' type of thing. We'd talk for a few months, hookup, then disappear again. We were both cool with it. He and I kept in touch and when I say kept in touch I mean I didn't delete his phone number. There wasn't much communication between us and if so, it was very sporadic.

This was within the first year of Malcolm and I dating, right after his accident when he was getting mean. Malcolm was bedridden at my parents' house. He'd take his pain meds with liquor to help him sleep through the pain, but drinking was like the mean potion. One of those nights he passed out drunk, I went to see Kris. My reason for cheating was always and still remains that it was simple. Kris was a straightforward dude and the relationship wasn't complexed. Malcolm was anything but plain, he was evil, and complicated, and confusing, and frustrating, and I just needed something simple, easy in my life. I don't remember who reached out to whom, but the type of dealing we had was easy to pick up and put down.

Also, it is important to note that to Malcolm cheating was the ABSOLUTE WORST THING you could do to another human being. Murder and rape are forgivable, but cheating? NO. He was loyal to a fault, so he used that narrative to make himself better than me. Malcolm used cheating as a measurement of worth or value. People who cheat are at the bottom. Malcolm was at the tippy top because he hadn't cheated. This was the first time I was afraid of him.

You know the old saying "What's done in the dark will come to the light." Let's just say I'm a firm believer of that cliche. There isn't really such a thing as a well-kept secret, and it was bound to come out eventually.

At my surprise 25th birthday party that Malcolm threw for me at my parents' house, he went through my phone and found evidence of the indiscretion. To this day, I never really understood why Malcolm chose this inopportune time to search through my phone. Nothing would ever be the same or go back to the way it was. I apologized and apologized and apologized, but Malcolm wanted me to suffer, to forever be indebted to him, to essentially kiss his entire ass in order to rebuild the trust that had been broken. I honestly don't remember the details of how it played out at my parents' house. Malcolm played it cool long enough to get me to himself. The war started when he had me isolated back home alone with him. Malcolm was WIDE OPEN and didn't spare me from his verbal lashing, 'whore', 'slut', 'bitch', 'liar', and 'cheater' were only some of the names he called me that day, and the beginning of language that would get much, much worse. Verbal jab after verbal jab, each feeling like a dagger cutting me to my core deeper with the impact of each word.

Malcolm forced me to call my sister on speaker phone to try to catch her in a lie. He made me call other people I had had dealings with in the past that he incorrectly assumed were still going on to again try and entrap me or them in a lie. Malcolm texted my friends and family to tell them how horrible of a person I was because I had cheated on him. The worst part of it was that he wanted EVERY SINGLE DAMN DETAIL of what happened. Malcolm pressured me to recount everything that happened leaving out no details. It was like Malcolm was interrogating me to find discrepancies in my account of the story. He wanted a play by play or highlight reel of all of my wrongs. Having to repeat and be put on public display sickened me to my core. I tried to explain that the details didn't matter, but nothing I said was heard. I tried to communicate to Malcolm that hearing all the descriptions of my indiscretions would only make it harder for him to heal but my words fell on deaf ears. Malcolm wanted to confront the man I had cheated with because he was convinced there was more to the story than what I was telling him. Again, he was wrong, but Malcolm in his mind was never ever wrong. NEVER.

This was the first time he put his ***hands on*** me too. After one of the setup calls, the one with my sister, I hung up the phone and Malcolm just violently slapped me across the face. Almost like he was manhandling an enemy. My neck snapped back suddenly from the impact. Placing my hand over my bruised cheek, I could literally feel Malcolm's fingerprints burning against the skin on my face. My cheek was hot and stinging from the impact of the slap Malcolm gave me. I didn't say or do anything. Just took it. I simply sat there.

Adding insult to my injury, Malcolm said I deserved to feel just some of the pain he was feeling. My face was blanked by Malcolm's fingerprints and the after-effects of a painful throbbing sensation, however, the further damage took place within my heart and soul. Malcolm wouldn't relent. Through bloodshot, teary eyes, Malcolm made me give him the intimate details over and over again, all the while becoming more and more angry…

At some point the argument transitioned to the kitchen. He went into the fridge for something (for a beer because drinking made him EVEN meaner if you can believe that). I must have hit a trigger with something I said. He repeatedly opened and slammed the doors shut, food was falling out, jars were broken from being knocked around. Malcolm eventually stopped when the door would no longer close because he had ruined it with all of the pounding. Malcolm continued on a rampage destroying pictures of us, my personal belongings mostly, and anything else that was in his path. This lasted for at least three days.

It was if he blacked out and the beast within took over. I cried more because after EVERY fight I was the one who had to clean up. The pain of being attacked and then held accountable for putting everything back into place was heavy. It was as if I was routinely setting up and breaking down the stage of my own knock out fight.

Imagine having to gather up all the pieces of broken items scattered and *shattered* throughout the house all the while having to prepare to go to work the next day. Once again, I was left cleaning up Malcolm's messes. I don't think I ever fully got all the jelly, ketchup, glass, mustard, and other condiments up from the kitchen floor. I can still recall the sweet and sour stench of everything inside of my refrigerator meshing together. Synoptic to the debris that stained our floor, the bond between Malcolm and I had been more sour than sweet and now the foundation of the relationship was rotten.

To top it all off, Malcolm demanded that I leave my phone at home that Monday so that he could rummage through it for misinformation I may not have conveyed. Even if I were a saint, who would want to be subject to that kind of treatment? Somehow guilt took its course and I agreed to leave it with

Malcolm. Despite the fact that Malcolm had my phone in his possession, he still called me at work every hour on the hour to drill me on the messages he had access to. I ended up having to leave the office that day because Malcolm threatened to come to my job and cause a scene.

When I arrived home, he destroyed my phone. Malcolm took my iPhone and shattered it as he proclaimed that I wasn't loyal.

Malcolm was now in full control of me and everything I was seemingly connected to. Demeaning me made Malcolm feel empowered. His hands were now all over me and not in the way that a woman would warrant.

## DOG IN THE FIGHT

I don't know if you've ever heard the following phrase used as a figure of speech as it relates to an individual's perspective of a conflict. ***"I don't have a dog in the fight."*** Usually this statement is used to portray the fact that one may not have a stake in the outcome.

Literally, my story was the opposite of this above phrase. Malcolm and I both literally and figuratively had a 90-pound strapping Pitbull consistently in the middle of our fights. I say our fights because although I was an unwilling participant, I was involved, nonetheless. Malcolm had a 90-pound Pitbull named King that I inherited in the relationship.

King was extremely protective over me as I was a caregiver to him just like I cared for his owner. One part of King was kind, protective, and gentle but the other side of him was fierce and focused. It seemed that King could always sense the tension between Malcolm and I. King would literally put his body or stand on his hind legs in order to create separation between Malcolm during the heat of argument. Can you imagine how tensed I was not knowing if King would go into attack mode? Would he choose to defend me or Malcolm? There were times I would have to deescalate King or put him away before things got out of hand.

There were several times that King saved my life and I don't say that loosely. King was truly a guard **dog**. I've discovered over the course of my life that often animals are more sensitive than humans. King picked up on everything that took place in the house and appeared to be the only one concerned about my safety or well-being.

The National Domestic Violence Hotline reports 43% of dating college women report experiencing violent and abusive dating behaviors including physical, sexual, tech, verbal or controlling abuse. I wish I could say I was exempt from these statistics but in all sincerity, I was stuck dead smack in the middle of them.

Six out of seven days a week, Malcolm would pick a fight with me. He thought it was a cute nickname to call me "Bri-atch." Brittany and bitch merged together. That was actually his term of endearment for me. Malcolm knew I hated being called a BITCH, so he would play on those words all the time. He'd revert to saying that I was acting like a BITCH. One day I had up to the brim with him calling me out of my name. An urge to retaliate came over me almost like the scene from the movie "What's Love Got To Do With It" starring Angela Bassett as Tina Turner. Just like Tina Turner fought back against her abuser, Ike Turner, I was prepared to do the same. Right after I asked Malcolm repeatedly to not call me out of my name, he yelled out to me, "You are acting like a BITCH" and before I knew it, I had put scissors to his neck. Holding the scissors firmly to pierce the skin Malcolm's neck I said, "You want me to be BITCH? I'll show you a bitch!"

He would rant daily about me not wanting to have sex with him. Why would I want to be intimate with a man who constantly beats me down? There would be times where I would constantly serve him mixed drinks in hopes that he would pass out drunk so the accusations and fussing would cease. Peace and rest from the verbal and occasional physical conflicts was all I wanted. There was never a time that Malcolm physically forced me to have sex, but there were many moments where I stared at the ceiling during intercourse hoping and praying it would be over soon. If I said no, it would spark an argument and the accusation about another affair on my end would begin. Malcolm felt because he hadn't cheated, he was held at a higher standard and had a free pass to wreck my life.

I'm about to share with you a very detailed account that makes my flesh crawl to this day have to recall it. You know that thing you think about it after you've survived that makes your eyes well up with tears and count your many blessings?

One night while I was in the bedroom, Malcolm began to yell at me as I was laying down on the floor. Malcolm proceeded to throw a glass in my direction that barely missed me and **shattered** against the wall nearby. Then Malcolm quickly approached me from behind and pounced on top of me shouting, "Since you want to act like a whore, I'll treat you like one!" Next Malcolm grabbed me from behind and began to thrust himself against me. He didn't penetrate me, but I still felt disgusted. He began to gyrate while yelling, "This is how you like! This how you wanted it! This is how you did it, whore!" I started to yell again and again at Malcolm to get off of me! Malcolm, you're hurting me! To no avail, Malcolm kept going until King ran upstairs being alarmed by the verbal exchange. King was barking hysterically and in attack mode. I did my best to remain calm while tears streamed down my cheeks. See, I was forced to keep my composure even in a violated position because I didn't want King to attack one of us. Eventually, I was able to settle King down and escape.

At that moment, I felt so filthy and degraded. A soapy shower wouldn't be able to rinse the imprint Malcolm left on me that night. Malcolm had taken it too far. I wasn't his girl toy. That was the longest 20 seconds of my life. Who knows what would have happened to me if I didn't have a dog in the fight.

## HIT THE PAVEMENT

Once I decided to play hooky from work and spend the day with Malcolm. We decided to jump in the car and headed to a nearby amusement park. The day was going according to plan and Malcolm and I were having fun. Malcolm and I spent the entire day riding rides and playing games.

Before heading back home, we decided to stop off and grab dinner at a local restaurant along the way. Dinner was great, and it was like a breath of fresh air to be having a good time with Malcolm. This was all about to change drastically.

On the drive home, Malcolm began to get extremely upset out of the blue. It was like Malcolm switched his mood and almost like he had a split personality. He began to fuss and blurt things at me. I couldn't believe how Malcolm was transforming before my eyes.

Malcolm pulls over on the side of the road and tells me to get out of the car. I am reluctant and in total shock that he would even think of abandoning me on the side of the road. I'm saying to myself this can't be happening. This must be a joke. At the time, I was recovering from an injury and my knee was in a brace. With that said, I wasn't taking him seriously until Malcolm came around the car to the passenger side and grabbed me. He proceeded to pull me out the car dragging me across the asphalt. The brace that covered my injured knee was scrapped and scuffed by the friction from the pavement. I suffered scratches on multiple parts of my body.

Malcolm treated me like roadkill, abandoned me in the thick of the evening, and sped away. I sat there on the side of the road sobbing until no more tears could be formed and my voice was gone. Truly, I didn't see this coming from a mile away. Malcolm had left me without a phone, no money, and without of a way to get home. In the midst of all the madness, I didn't have time to retrieve my purse from the backseat of Malcolm's vehicle.

The feeling of loneliness and abandonment immediately came over me but before it could fully settle, I was interrupted. A lady and her husband approached me and happened to have witnessed the entire account of what happened. I don't know if you believe in miracles by angels dwelling among us. The two people that saw me on the side of the road were nothing short of a sign from God. They did the miraculous for me that night.

They offered to help me and ask me if there was anyone else I could call to pick me up. Immediately, my mind went to my sister. I used the phone they provided to call my sister. When my sister answered the phone, I briefly explained the events that occurred through tears. My sister left right away to pick me up. The couple stayed with me and offered their support until my sister arrived. Truly, I don't know where I would have been if they didn't display some random acts of kindness.

Once my sister arrived, I crawled into the car and headed home back to the house. My sister was still living at home with my dad so staying with her wasn't an option. By the time I got to the house, Malcolm was asleep, and I went inside battered, rejected, abused and hurt. I dreaded (with every fiber of my being) having to go back to the house after Malcolm treated me worse than the scum of the earth. There was nowhere else to go. I hear you on the other side of the page saying to yourself there is always somewhere else to go. I wouldn't have taken that. Trust me, I hear you loud and clear now, but back then, I was stuck between a rock and harder place.

# REFLECTIONS

**(Feel free to journal your thoughts and learning experiences by answering the questions below).**

HOW DID YOU FEEL WHEN READING THIS CHAPTER?

_____

_____

_____

_____

_____

WHAT DID YOU LEARN?

_____

_____

_____

_____

_____

HOW CAN YOU USE THIS INFORMATION TO HELP SOMEONE ELSE IN LIFE?

_____

_____

_____

_____

_____


HOW DOES THE CONTENT OF THIS CHAPTER RELATE TO YOUR LIFE EXPERIENCE(S)?

_____

_____

_____

_____

_____

# CHAPTER 6

⟨↬⟩

# MESS ON THE LAWN

It was always emphasized by my parents that what happens inside of the house stays inside of the home. As mentioned beforehand, I was groomed to grin and bear whatever came my way. So, the stage was already set for me to keep all of the *mess* that Malcolm and I were going through tucked in neatly behind my smile and pleasant demeanor.

I'd become great at suppressing my feelings and emotions and living behind the mask I created for years. The flip side of holding everything in is the velocity of the thing you're suppressing rising to the top. See, up until this point, life had prepared me to implode, but I had no real-life experience of how to cope when things explode.

Not long after Malcolm and I moved into his place, things got extremely messy because it truly never really felt like my home. After the affair was the very first time I attempted to stand up to Malcolm. I took full responsibility for my actions, but I also felt that his reaction was not normal. Observing Malcolm's temperament, I informed him I was going to my parents' house until he calmed down. CUE MELTDOWN! Zero to sixty! Malcolm called my dad and cursed my name and told him I wasn't welcome at the house anymore and to come get me before he did something worse. Go figure that Malcolm had no hesitation to shame me in front of my parents. Malcolm was extremely bold and blunt.

My parents lived maybe 20 minutes away and it was the longest 20 minutes of my life. I felt like it was hours instead of minutes. Malcolm grew more and more impatient by the second. Malcolm couldn't wait to put me out. While we were marking time, Malcolm literally threw me out. Malcolm collected everything I had there and threw it out of the front door. Clothes, makeup, school books, jewelry… all tossed out on the front **lawn**…in the dirt. It was almost as if my personal belongings being sprawled out the front yard portrayed the context of my relationship with Malcolm. Parts of me were scattered and out of sort. What was on the inside of me was now being revealed outwardly.

There was nothing I could do but watch. Malcolm was furious and irate. He was always angry with me. I was left on the outside to look in. Malcolm continued to call me names and threaten me even once my parents arrived. Unfortunately, Malcolm couldn't turn his behaviors on and off. I believe he didn't know anything about self-control.

Shocked by Malcolm's erratic behavior, my mom and dad calmly collected my stuff off the front lawn and took me back to their house. No one confronted him for his behavior. No one said much leaving the house that day. The car was full of silence, the type of quiet where all that interrupts is the sound of the engine running.

A moment that ranks extremely high on my list of regrets. No one EVER stood up to Malcolm and I had learned it the hard way. I felt helpless and defenseless. I had no defenders. My dad and mom said nothing. It was like Malcolm was given a free pass to continue to wreck my life while everyone that I assumed cared stood by and watched.

At my parent's house, my mother and father were abnormally distant. I felt more like they were giving me room to figure it out on my own, not so much that they were being neglectful. They had a 'didn't know what to say, so they didn't say anything' type of vibe. This was the time I needed my mom and dad the most. Truly, I needed them to communicate with me. Deep inside, I yearned for my parents to say something that could soothe the pain I was feeling. Have you ever felt as if you were standing in a room full of trapped doors? At that instance in time, that was the feeling I had and felt there was no exit in sight. The longing in my heart for communication was met head on by the rebuttal of silence. My mom and dad didn't ask questions, or offer suggestions, they just left me alone to be sad.

## GARBAGE BAGS

I remember looking around the room as my eyes started to fixate on several bags nearby that I'd manage to bring with me. As I opened the garbage bags (one by one) that my stuff was in, I died more on the inside. Everything was ruined. All of my personal belongings were now defective. Either *shattered* or damaged somehow. Malcolm had accomplished what he set out to do to me. Malcolm sought to destroy all that I loved when he didn't get his way or lost control. Ironically, my life at that point felt stuffed into the confines of Malcolm's garbage bags. All that was attached to me personally was being fragmented. It was hard, too difficult to breathe in that relationship and I was treated beyond words that day. He claimed to value me sooo much, so it did feel like I was a treasure, but one that was locked away.

Far from perfect but knew within myself I deserved better. I was in so much pain as I reflected on what I had gotten myself into and the situation I'd been put in. Now all of my business was literally out in the street.

STUPID me.....I went back. Backwards I went.

On average, a woman will flee an abusive relationship seven times before she leaves for good according to The National Domestic Violence Hotline. This was one of the times.

Life went downhill from here…

Malcolm is a textbook narcissist, arrogant and controlling in all relationships, insecure and unaware of his own realities. Like I said before, the injury brought out all the worst sides of Malcolm and because we were in a new house alone together the next few years, I would be a victim of his anger for years to come. Malcolm had me in the vices of a tight grip. He had secured the bag. Malcolm first isolated me from my friends and family. He said they influenced me when I had cheated previously, and he didn't like me being around them. So okay! I'd do anything to fix the trust between him and I. I can step back from friends and family for the sake of the relationship, no problem. The next thing he controlled was where I went and how I dressed. Malcolm felt uncomfortable with me being around people I had previously dated because I had proven that my self-control was weak. Malcolm didn't mind throwing me away but didn't want anyone else to have me.

# REFLECTIONS

**(Feel free to journal your thoughts and learning experiences by answering the questions below).**

### HOW DID YOU FEEL WHEN READING THIS CHAPTER?

_____

_____

_____

_____

_____

### WHAT DID YOU LEARN?

_____

_____

_____

_____

_____

HOW CAN YOU USE THIS INFORMATION TO HELP SOMEONE ELSE IN LIFE?

_____

_____

_____

_____

_____

HOW DOES THE CONTENT OF THIS CHAPTER RELATE TO YOUR LIFE EXPERIENCE(S)?

_____

_____

_____

_____

# CHAPTER 7

# I DO

## THE PROPOSAL

*I Do* is the vow of endearment we make to our spouses on our wedding day and most affectionately to our soulmates. A wedding can only properly begin after a ***proposal*** is made. Typically, at the conclusion of a ***proposal*** from the man you love, it is custom to respond to the question of 'will you marry me?' Normally, there is a rush of joyous emotions that flood the hearts of the bride-to-be. Often tears of joy, physical affection, and warm and fuzzy feelings encompass or accompany the moment surrounding an engagement.

Malcolm's proposal was far from typical, although it was definitely unexpected. December 15, 2013, I recall it well being the morning of my dance recital. I was up early frantically trying to locate my makeup brushes, costume, and other pertinent things needed for my dance performance. Malcolm was acting extremely obnoxious that morning. He kept on standing in my way and demanding me to locate things for him, knowing I had a deadline and a time to be at the recital. The more he asked me for things, the more I became annoyed and told him to get what he wanted himself. I was heated by Malcolm's continuous nagging and couldn't wait to collect my things and head out of the house.

Walking around in my robe prior to me getting dressed, I attempted to collect everything I needed as I passed by Malcolm downstairs. Standing beside the coffee table in the living room, I turned around and to my surprise, Malcolm was kneeling on one knee with a ring in his hands. My mouth opened wide, but I was really confused at the same time. Malcolm was speaking, but I heard no words at all as if the sound had been unplugged to a movie I was watching. I just looked at him and the only thing I could see in that instance was Malcolm's mouth moving. My mind drifted away like an out of body experience. Was this really happening after all of the painful words and our traumatic past and present? Why would you want to marry this whore you called me every day? How could Malcolm wait until I was irritated before he asked me to marry him? Was Malcolm playing a trick on me?

At the moment Malcolm proposed, I have no recollection of all the thoughts that went through my mind. To be honest, I did feel a sense of excitement because it was flattering to be proposed to by Malcolm. So, I managed to flail my hands in the air and scream oh my God, oh my God! Yes! Yes! Malcolm slid the ring onto my finger.

I do remember the tenseness in my body as I said yes. I said yes to Malcolm because I was asked and that is what I was supposed to do. Yes was my response because I wanted to right a wrong I'd done. Saying yes to Malcolm felt like untying a knot of mistakes and hoped it would provide a reset on our relationship.

When I arrived at the recital, I met my mom and sister there. I flashed my ring to them and proceeded to tell them what had happened. Before I could get the entire story out, my mom and sister interrupted me by saying, "Malcolm did it early. We can't believe he did it beforehand." My sister and my mom went on to explain that Malcolm had planned to ask me to marry him on centerstage at my recital. Thank God that didn't happen. Malcolm stayed true to script and spontaneously decided not to wait and proposed to me at home. Malcolm was known to make plans and change them within a moment's pause without letting anyone else know. So, my family wasn't able to be a part of the proposal at all after being informed of the plan.

## THE WEDDING

To no avail, my yes to the ***proposal*** wouldn't change a thing. Back home, it was worse, nothing I did was ever good enough. I was still called every name under the sun. There were holes in the wall and broken furniture everywhere from when Malcolm lost his temper because he said he'd never hit me, but that didn't stop him from smashing anything he could get his hands on in my vicinity. The house was a battlefield.

We were required to do premarital counseling prior to getting married and it uncovered a lot of flaws in Malcolm's character that he had never had to face. I strongly believe that this was the first time Malcolm even came close to looking at a reflection of himself in the mirror. During one of the sessions when the facilitating premarital counseling pastor addressed the abuse within the relationship, Malcolm became beyond livid. Looking in from the outside, it was as if Malcolm's blood began to boil and he and the pastor almost went to blows. I was so afraid and thought a fight was going to break out right there in the office. Malcolm vowed never to come back to counseling and of course he blamed me. However, Malcolm was forced to return because the pastor informed him that he wouldn't officiate our wedding unless we finished. Malcolm reluctantly obliged.

During this time, the wedding plans were well underway. My

godmother and her sister took over the coordination of the wedding. They were much more religion based than I, and much more conservative. With that said, the wedding plans were super traditional, although I appreciate them for doing their best.

It took us six months to plan the entire wedding. Most of the time, I'd ask Malcolm how he wanted to be included and he said nothing but complained and accused me later of making the wedding all about me. He barely paid for anything and didn't help at all with the planning. Malcolm would say, "You want this wedding to be all about you. You're just an attention whore." The truth be told, nothing involving the wedding was about me.

The wedding was nice, and everyone went on about how beautiful it was, but it wasn't what I truly wanted. On the outside, it was a sight to see. My friends and loved ones raved over how I was such a beautiful bride, although I was internally dying inside without life support.

Despite the roller coaster relationship I'd been having with my father due to his infidelity, I still decided to have him walk me down the aisle and give me away. Truly, I felt it was the right thing to do. After all, he introduced me to Malcolm, and he was still my father. Trust me, we all make mistakes.

I desired a celebratory atmosphere because I knew Malcolm and I liked to party. The wedding was conservative to say the least, but it wasn't inside of a church.

Due to the wedding being arranged under religious guidelines, a party atmosphere didn't happen. No drinking. No partying. Six months had come and gone, I said *I do,* and we were Mr. & Mrs.

## THE HONEYMOON

Honeymoons are usually sweet spots and the icing on the wedding cake. I was really excited and looked forward to getting away and being out of the country for the first time. In my mind, the honeymoon was going to be the bright spot of it all. Just maybe I could have this fairytale ending most women dream of and leave this present nightmare behind me. I hoped being married to Malcolm would spark a new beginning and bring us closer. Perhaps we could put all of the past in our rearview mirrors. Besides, we stood eye to eye before a crowd of witnesses and said *I Do* until death do us part.

So much for wishful thinking. We hadn't even reached our destination before Malcolm started showing signs of his true colors. On the flight, Malcolm voiced that I wasn't paying any attention to him and that I was more concerned with the scenery. Like the countless others that have flown for the first time, I was very intrigued at the sites around me. Instead of experiencing that life moment with me, he sought to bring me back into his realm of negativity. We were 30,000 feet in the air, newly married, and sitting next to each other, and I was once again having to defend myself. The excitement about the trip instantly sucked out of me like a parasite does to its host. Malcolm and I hadn't arrived on our honeymoon and it was already feeling like home.

After the flight, he really let loose. We landed in Mexico for an eight-day honeymoon. Malcolm had proven that his temper couldn't be tamed. It was more like a hellamoon instead of a honeymoon.

I spent days one to four days crying because – well, Malcolm was simply being himself: mean, accusatory, angry, narcissistic and unforgiving. Who spends their honeymoon in horror and agony? Our first days as newlyweds were repeat episodes of all the years before. The honeymoon further proved that Malcolm's ill treatment had no boundaries. Quickly I was rudely awakened to the fact that being Malcolm's wife didn't change a thing and he still had a target on my back. My *I Do* meant nothing to Malcolm.

# REFLECTIONS

**(Feel free to journal your thoughts and learning experiences by answering the questions below).**

HOW DID YOU FEEL WHEN READING THIS CHAPTER?

_____

_____

_____

_____

_____

WHAT DID YOU LEARN?

_____

_____

_____

_____

_____

HOW CAN YOU USE THIS INFORMATION TO HELP SOMEONE ELSE IN LIFE?

_____

_____

_____

_____

_____

HOW DOES THE CONTENT OF THIS CHAPTER RELATE TO YOUR LIFE EXPERIENCE(S)?

_____

_____

_____

_____

_____

# CHAPTER 8

# FIRE ALARM

Can you reach back in time and capture a memory of an instance where you found yourself doing something and the sound of an alarm interrupted it? Maybe it was in a classroom setting where you were busy working on a task and the fire alarm triggered a sound that disturbed you and the entire class. Following the alarm, you with a sense of urgency had to drop everything you were doing to exit the building most likely in a single-file line. The first time it happened you were made aware that the *fire alarm* was just a precaution or a drill. The more and more the alarm sounded, the more acquainted you became with it. Little by little, the alarm didn't disturb you as much as it did the first time. Before you realized it, the resound became like second nature because you had become desensitized by it. I strongly believe the same can be said in abusive relationships. The more I heard the alarms warning me to get out of this toxic relationship with Malcolm, the more familiar I got comfortable inside of it. Oblivious to the fact that the longer I stayed, the lower the alarm of my conscious urging me to leave would sound. Some of you reading this page know all too well what I'm referring to in this sentence.

Throughout my relationship with Malcolm, everything around me was speaking or foretelling me to end it and seek to become my better self. Even the chain of events that were occurring at the house in which Malcolm and I lived depicted where we were in our relationship. It's mind blowing how the answer to our questions and the solutions to our problems can be hidden in plain sight.

For example, Malcolm had a power cord that was the big wrap-around kind. It was plugged into something and I can't remember what device. Malcolm was in the bed and unable to walk at the time and it caught on fire. I was unable to move him to safety or put out the fire, so I called 911 for assistance.

Remember King was extremely protective, so he didn't let anyone in the house. When the firemen showed up, I was pulling him off his front legs to let these men in the house so that they could come assess the fire.

The firemen had to come, and I had to hold back King (90-pound pit bull) and he could barely get down the steps to get out the house because the firemen needed to check for further hazards. The house never really caught fire, just smoked a lot. I got it unplugged which stopped it from sparking. It was always something. Always something speaking out to me from the distance telling me to get the hell out. I simply ignored the signs. I later realized that it wasn't my responsibility to rescue Malcolm and whatever I had done didn't warrant me being destroyed because of it. The fire was sparked by a faulty cord and bad connection. Just like my union with Malcolm, our relationship came about by a faulty connection. Our relationship was in knots and burning the very life out of me. Time and time again, the alarm bells were ringing, but I had become used to sound.

## FALSE ALARM

These were some of the little warnings that didn't quite blow up yet. In today's time, these are considered *false alarms*. The carpet was burnt after that. All of this occurred less than 90 days after we had moved in.

Another thing in the relationship that alarmed me was our sex life. As a direct result of how Malcolm treated me, I was completely turned off. Sex was another reason he would get mad at me. He was so nasty to me, so I had ZERO physical attraction towards him, but then that was just fuel to the fire. Malcolm constantly accused me of cheating. He would get so angry when I didn't want to be intimate. My options were to grin and bear it, or be fussed at, interrogated, and name called for hours after that. This was alarming to me and left me feeling empty or like a dumping ground. Intimately, there was no connection outside of physical presence between Malcolm and me. Although he never forced himself on me physically, there were countless times I stared into space or the top of the ceiling praying that the exchange would be over soon. Many nights after intercourse, I felt the void of being unloved, undervalued, and unappreciated. Several nights were spent wetting my pillow with silent tears as I drowned out the internal sirens urging me to cry out for help.

Many human service clinicians and professionals often refer to this as phase one and two in the abuse cycle. "**Phase 1 and 2:** The first and second phases are where the victim starts to not regard or care for their abuser anymore and disconnects emotionally and mentally from the abusive relationship" (*National Domestic Violence Hotline Resource Guide*).

I was right smack in the middle of this phase at that time.

All of the bottled-up emotions trapped inside me were bound to come to a head. I began to implode. I could no longer silence the alarms in my head. Daily, I battled depression and anxiety not knowing how the day would play out or what would set Malcolm off.

I was at my low point. I had nothing left, and Malcolm had finally succeeded in breaking my spirit. I cried daily. I'd hide in the closet while he yelled at me through the door. I kept a blunt object near the bed at night because I feared for my safety when he would lash out. I'd intentionally work late just so I didn't have to be home with Malcolm. My life was ***shattered.*** All of these feelings erupting on the inside of me led to my suicide attempt. One day, like a glass that had too much poured into it, I overflowed. No longer could I mask the pain or pretend it didn't exist. I couldn't tuck my broken heart in any longer. It was time to take matters into my own hands. I knew where Malcolm's pain pills were and wanted my hurt to stop. To be completely transparent, I wanted the never-ending cycle of pain to come to a halt and I didn't care how. Approaching the medicine cabinet full of prescribed narcotics, I gathered all of the bottles of opioids from the upstairs cabinet. I took a handful of them at first. A way of escape is what I longed for and I did not know how to get free. I needed an outlet, a way out of no way. Swallowing the opioids one by one and some by the fist full until I'd taken them all. I didn't want to die. I simply wanted to rest. If I end my suffering before he kills me, I'd get away from Malcolm. See, I was on the underside of rock bottom. I was sad, dismayed, and just longed for sleep.

No one would have to know, and it seemed as if no one cared at that time. Before I knew it, I drifted off to sleep. The medicine I'd taken had put me under but had failed to take me out. I woke up many hours later sick as a dog. The side effects of all the opioids I'd ingested were turning my stomach inside out, but I was still alive. I didn't go to the emergency room although I should have. I spent the next two days puking my guts out. Sick but I was alive. Broken but in the land of the living, nonetheless.

To add further insult to my injury, Malcolm didn't even notice anything was going on with me. Like always, Malcolm was only consumed with himself. Malcolm just thought I was sick and because I didn't have to report into work at the time, I was able to keep the suicide attempt under wraps.

This was the first time I listened to the *alarm* ringing out to me. I was thinking to myself after all has been said and done. I was now in **Phase 3**. The third phase includes becoming aware of the repercussions of the abuse. In the third phase, the abused begins to make preparations to leave" (*National Domestic Violence Hotline Resource Guide).*

I said the following inwardly: If I don't manage to get out of this situation, **I'LL DIE HERE**. I thank God it was just a *false alarm* and I did not end my life by accident.

# REFLECTIONS

**(Feel free to journal your thoughts and learning experiences by answering the questions below).**

HOW DID YOU FEEL WHEN READING THIS CHAPTER?

_____

_____

_____

_____

_____

WHAT DID YOU LEARN?

_____

_____

_____

_____

_____

HOW CAN YOU USE THIS INFORMATION TO HELP SOMEONE ELSE IN LIFE?

_____

_____

_____

_____

_____

HOW DOES THE CONTENT OF THIS CHAPTER RELATE TO YOUR LIFE EXPERIENCE(S)?

_____

_____

_____

_____

_____

# CHAPTER 9

❦

# HOUSE ON FIRE

Fire inside of a fireplace can heat and provide comfort for an entire home. The same fire can destroy an entire **house** from the inside out if left burning uncontrollably. The key to destruction or bliss is sometimes measured by a fine line. Too far to the left or right can make the world of difference. It is critical to note that relationships can be severed or repaired merely with the slightest of adjustments.

Things with Malcolm and I had been heating up for years. Our relationship was on *fire* by then and not the way most people would interpret it. When I say *fire*, I'm not referring to burning passion, love, or intimacy that should be radiating throughout a healthy marriage. We were constantly heated with each other and almost each day was built around recurring conflicts. Picture in your head living in the house with someone with friction all around you and never being able to anticipate when a *fire* would strike. I wasn't just walking on pins and needles with Malcolm. It was more like walking on hot coals and I was long over being burned repeatedly.

**LIFELINE**

Every so often in life, God gives you an opportunity to show you that He is still with you in the *fire.* I had failed to realize at first that I'd already been given a *lifeline.* Remember when I told you that

Malcolm and I were mandated to attend counseling prior to getting married? As aforementioned, it uncovered a lot of flaws in Malcolm's character that he had never had to face, and he blamed me for it. Well, from the counseling session I became close with the preacher and first lady (an abuse counselor). When the abuse was referred to as 'abuse' the first time, I remember feeling all the blood drain from my body. I had been living in an abusive relationship, I had married my abuser, I made less than $20k a year, and Malcolm was NEVER going to let me just leave.

"**Phase 4:** The fourth phase is returning to the relationship. Phase 4 includes a lot of back and forth. The abused need a clear understanding, but they also desire to be physically, mentally and emotionally connected again, which coerces them into going back to the relationship" (***National Domestic Violence Hotline Resource Guide).*** This phase clearly illustrates why I would come back to Malcolm once I left previously.

I somehow managed to keep in touch with the First Lady, the wife of the pastor who provided our premarital counseling. She was worried about me because she saw all the warning signs, so she helped me plan my exit. The First Lady threw me a *lifeline* and I took it.

I had to be strategic. Leaving wasn't going to be easy and staying gone I knew would be the hardest. Over the next few weeks, I collected whatever cash I could without Malcolm noticing. I gathered essentials and hid them in the trunk of my car. My heart would pound in fear like a battle drum each time I made a move towards freedom. At that time, I concealed things in a secure place that I could access quickly just in case that day was going to be the day I used my *lifeline*. I am so grateful that someone had the foresight to think on my behalf, and for once, in my best interest.

The First Lady was helping me retrain my mind and extending me enough rope to grab a hold to a new life. I'm forever indebted to her and can't thank her enough.

One weekend, Malcolm and I were binge watching the Star Wars movies since it was a long Labor Day weekend. We had gotten to episode three and Malcolm just snapped. Out of nowhere, Malcolm started drilling me on my comings and goings, demanded to go through my phone, and he wanted to see my bank statements for proof of spending. To this day, I don't know what triggered Malcolm because he had so many triggers and I was usually pretty good at flying under his radar.

As he fussed, I saw my life. I was his lap dog, a pet. He wanted me to sit at his feet and be a good little puppy until he was ready to play with me. We'd go out, there were fun times, but he was always in control, and I would never get to live for myself. I was allowing Malcolm to live and thrive vicariously through me almost like he was my puppet master with strings attached. That Sunday morning, **September 7, 2015**, I ran. That seventh day in September will always be both a milestone and a memorial. I decided to use my *lifeline.* That day, I wanted to live more than die. In my pajamas I stood up without saying a word and before Malcolm realized what was happening, I had my keys and purse in hand. Everything I needed was already prepared. I went to my car and drove off. It would take forever to describe how I felt or to put into words what was going through my mind as I pulled off. My palms were sweaty and heart was racing, yet a calm of determination kept me focused on leaving.

Malcolm repeatedly called, texted, and voice messaged. I cried and cried and cried and cried, and then I cried some more. I went to my mom's house, eyes bloodshot and drained from the escape. My phone rang nonstop. How dare I leave Malcolm? Then the texts started. "Selfish, evil, liar, manipulator, user, bitch, whore." Malcolm posted it on Facebook, and he texted my closest friends trying to get a reaction from me. That was the longest night of my life. Yet I didn't respond. I was focused on my *lifeline.*

I barely slept that night. I was afraid Malcolm would show up at my mom's house. The next morning my mom and I went to the police station to get a restraining order because – guess what? – there's no help for abuse victims until AFTER something happens. To my demise, it was Labor Day weekend, and everything was closed on Monday. By now, I had blocked his calls and texts and it was too hurtful to see. So, he started sending emails. In a last-ditch effort to just get him to stop, I told his mom that I was reporting the abuse to his commanding officer (he was still military) which halted him for the day. He was worried about how he'd look if his peers found out the type of man he REALLY was. Sad but true. Thank goodness for THAT insecurity. I filed a restraining order as soon as I was able to after that. I was finally free and never going back, but the hard part had just begun... I had to adjust to being free physically and mentally. Years of abuse wasn't something I wasn't going to just wash off with a hot shower. It was going to be a journey.

## HOUSE BURNING

Malcolm always used to say this to me. "I can't trust you. You might burn my house down." The house was in his name. Malcolm had summer training out of state. I wanted my brother to stay at the house with me while he was home from school for the summer. His biggest justification for not wanting my brother there was that he and I were not responsible enough to be left alone. His best example was since I didn't have any stake in the home, I would be reckless and possibly burn it down.

Ironically, Malcolm burned his own house down by accident. The neighbors saw it, and the dogs were going crazy.

One of the most frequently used passages of the scripture states: "If a house is divided against itself, that house cannot stand. I discovered that the house represented our relationship. The destructive dynamics and faulty foundation the union was built upon was destined to be destroyed from within. Just like the actual house burned down, the relationship went up in FLAMES. Although I played my role in the house, I didn't burn it down. Malcolm did.

The house and relationship were built on toxicity. That was tragic and not good for either of one of us. It's not just that I was being abused, Malcolm was actually in an abusive situation with himself. He didn't get the help that he needed.

Like anyone who finds themselves trapped inside a house that's on *fire,* instinct kicks in and they go into survival mode. I almost died in that house with Malcolm. I'd given all I could give as a woman and could no longer fan the flames of my abuser. I chose me. Decided to give myself a *lifeline*.

# REFLECTIONS

**(Feel free to journal your thoughts and learning experiences by answering the questions below).**

HOW DID YOU FEEL WHEN READING THIS CHAPTER?

_____

_____

_____

_____

_____

WHAT DID YOU LEARN?

_____

_____

_____

_____

_____

HOW CAN YOU USE THIS INFORMATION TO HELP SOMEONE ELSE IN LIFE?

_____

_____

_____

_____

_____

HOW DOES THE CONTENT OF THIS CHAPTER RELATE TO YOUR LIFE EXPERIENCE(S)?

_____

_____

_____

_____

_____

# CHAPTER 10

✑

# BACK FROM PIECES

## REALIZE YOU'RE BROKEN

Leaving Malcolm was merely the first baby steps to my transition. At the time I ran, I was prepared to leave, and my mind was made up but not returning was going to be my greatest obstacle yet. In self-examining my life with Malcolm under a microscope, I'd left him several times before, but kept returning through the revolving door of abuse. It was like there was a magnetic force field propelling me back to Malcolm. To put it another way, the cycle of abuse I underwent with Malcolm felt like the pulling of a rubber band that snaps or smacks your fingers back into place after you have stretched it to the greatest capacity. Imagine the sting.

It is effortless to neglect that women or men can still love or care for their abusers despite leaving them. In varying instances, love or affection for an abuser depicts an impactful role in going back.

I've discovered that doing the right thing is often just as painful and adhering to the wrong in your life. To be clear, I never want to paint a picture that leaving Malcolm was easy breezy, that everything was all bad, that I didn't love him, that I didn't care about his well-being, and that there wasn't some sick twisted sense of safety staying put. I questioned doing the right thing despite the reality that I knew leaving was the right thing to do. I wept a lot in the process of recovery. Malcolm and I had been together for years. The harsh reality I had to come to grips with was I'd have to leave *pieces* of my old self behind. Parts of me will never be restored, but often we have to shed old skin to grow the new. I had given Malcolm my body, soul, heart, and the most precious gem known to man – time. On the other hand, I'd received *pieces* of Malcolm's past and that cut and destroyed me to the core.

## REALIZE YOU'RE BROKEN

The more time I spent outside of the abuse, the more I saw my brokenness. It is imperative to note I wish I could say that I cut all ties with Malcolm overnight, but that would be far from the truth.

"**Phase 5:** Fifth phase is actually exiting an abusive union or relationship. Being away for half a year or more highlights this final phase.

It is difficult to leave an abusive relationship, and actually leaving will be one of the strongest things you will ever do. It takes time to leave for good, and if you're stuck in one of these stages, it is okay. That's what we're here for – to help you along the way.

Let's focus on the fourth stage, going back to the abusive relationship. Ultimately, the goal would be to skip this step altogether, and have only four stages in this process. However, even if this stage can't be eliminated, we will do our best to reduce the number of times that survivors return to abusers. In order to do this, we will explore different reasons why survivors of domestic violence return to these relationships. Once we understand why people go back, we will know what is necessary to combat it" *(National Domestic Violence Hotline Resource Guide).*

Malcolm tried to reconcile the marriage for nine months to no avail. I refused to move back in because I discerned that nothing had really changed. Different day, but the same old Malcolm. Despite the fact that Malcolm was doing his darndest to mask his ways, the old rude and surly Malcolm would appear similar to a scene from the Incredible Hulk once he got angry. Malcolm went to counseling and his therapist called him a narcissist and then he terminated after that.

Needless to say, it wasn't a hard cut off. It was a weaning process. After the months of back and forth was over, I called it quits for good. Coming to terms with the fact that our relationship was **broken** beyond repair was eye opening and painful at the same time. I had to ask myself over and over if there was anything salvageable in the relationship. The only answer that kept coming to mind when asking the question of what could be saved in the relationship was me.

Informing Malcolm that I wanted to move the remaining items that were left from the house was no easy task. When my mother and brother showed up to the house, Malcolm caused a huge scene. Malcolm wouldn't let anyone in the house to help me move except my mom and watched us struggle to load heavy things while he wouldn't let my brother inside. Malcolm would rather two women wrestle with heavy furniture than to allow my brother to help. Malcolm's actions further solidified the end of our relationship and provided an open display of the kind of man he was.

## BACK TOGETHER

Over the next few months, I spent a lot of time reflecting and strategizing my next move. I needed to piece my life *back* together. Jotting my goals and future aspirations down inside my journal, I set out to accomplish them one at time. Each day that passed by, I learned to love myself a little more than the day before. I fell in love with this beautiful woman that starred innocently back at me in the mirror. It had been a long time since I saw me without a reflection of Malcolm. Through strong determination, as well as taking ownership over what I could own and releasing the chain of events beyond my control, I no longer wanted to be a victim. I slipped on my BIG GIRL PANTIES. No longer did I want to share or relinquish the power of my self-worth with Malcolm or anyone else for that matter. Taking the opportunity on this new lease on life, I set out to raise the bar higher.

For years I felt like I'd been divided from myself as a hold and that pieces of me had been scattered all over the place. I didn't feel centered or grounded where I felt I needed a new beginning.

Pursuing a change of pace, I moved to Lynchburg, Virginia in order to get back on my feet. Soon I found a job and started a new career. It is amazing what you can accomplish when you come *back* to who you really are. Slowly but steadily the tide of my life was changing, and the wind was blowing in my favor. The steps I began to take on a consistent basis transformed into strides and before long I was leaping into a better life.

Eventually, I hired a lawyer and filed for a divorce from Malcolm. Of course, Malcolm refused to sign the divorce under the pretense that he wasn't in agreement with it. It took three and a half years to divorce Malcolm, but it was finally complete. I felt alive again and had officially bounced back from *broken*.

## TELL IT

Throughout my history of abuse, I was unable to tell my truth because I thought holding it in was the right thing to do. I suffered in silence for so many years when I could have told someone. All I had to do was open my mouth and ***Tell It.*** Help is always there if we access it. Holding the abuser unaccountable causes the pain inside to perpetuate a cycle. Staying quiet won't stop the abuse.

"**Hope that things will change:** Abuse is a cycle with outbursts followed by apologies and a period of time in which the abuser tries to convince their partner that they can change, and it won't happen again. Because abusers aren't abusive all of the time, hope that the abuser will change can drive someone back.

**How do you move past this and stay away?**

Considering counseling can be a good step if you've known abuse most of your life. Matching yourself with a counselor can provide a safe and private environment for you to express your thoughts, feelings and fears. A counselor won't judge you and will be able to help you work through your past abuse and learn that it shouldn't be your normal. Entering counseling does not mean that you are mentally ill or cannot handle things on your own. What it does mean is that you are prioritizing your healing and succeeding and putting yourself in a position to do that. You can also work to educate yourself. The more you know about abuse, the less likely you are to think of it as normal, and you will be able to recognize abusive behaviors and stay away" *(**National Domestic Violence Hotline Resource Guide**)*.

If you are reading this page at this very moment and have suffered any type of abuse, there is hope and I'm throwing you a lifeline. ***Tell It.***

Refuse to keep your abuser's secret. Stop being quiet. Say something. Speak out against abuse. Don't be like me and wait for years when you could begin your journey to freedom today. I'm encouraging you or anyone else experiencing abuse to own their truth and put themselves first. Trust me, I know that's easier said than done, but it's not impossible. You don't have to endure stranglehold(s) of abuse while putting your voice on mute.

When I knew I wanted to share my story with the world, I was and still am nervous about it. I was also embarrassed to a point because I felt like I let myself and others down. However, I shifted my mentality to realize it wasn't my fault no matter what transpired in the relationship. Say this with me: **I AM NOT THE CAUSE OF THE ABUSE I'VE SUFFERED!**

I remember when I was contemplating sharing my story with the world. I was inspired by a college mate who shared her story of being abused openly. My classmate even established a GoFundMe page in order to raise funds and awareness of domestic violence. Hearing my classmate's story gave me the motivation I needed. We combat abuse together as a community.

Upon my escape from brokenness, many I come into contact with have asked me questions around my process. I am beyond blessed to be alive to share with you some intimate details that are outlined in the questions and answers noted below.

## 1 - What did the abuse feel like?

I never understood what was happening. I didn't even know it was abuse, I had no idea actually. I thought it was supposed to be that way. I was confused a lot. "What did I do wrong now?" was the question I asked myself constantly. I felt like he was trying to break me daily. If I said the sky was blue, he'd fuss at me for hours about how I was wrong and selfish, and it just confused me. I didn't understand how the blue sky made me a selfish person. It was frustrating because I am a very logical person and none of what he said or did ever made sense. He was hurt that I cheated but wanted every dirty detail. He said I was selfish but everything that happened under that roof was about him. He said I was a liar, but I wasn't lying. Confusion was the first layer of emotion and then frustration.

I beat myself up about it a lot too. I am very much an achiever, so I felt I was the reason my relationship and marriage were failing. It was like a double whammy. I'm sad AND I'm being mistreated. I blamed myself.

## 2 – List details of why you stayed.

I stayed because we were married and that's what you're "supposed to do." Fight for your relationship. I stayed because I didn't know there was another option. I stayed because I had no money to leave, and if he found out I was saving or planning to leave, it would have been a million times worse because he would have forced me to stop somehow. It was ALL mental. He wanted to break me down to nothing so he could control me. I stayed because I was embarrassed of admitting to a failed marriage less than a year after being married. I stayed because I had no support. My parents had split up after my dad had an affair. My mom was living with her sister and sister's boyfriend in my grandma's old house. I had nowhere to go, no money to get there, and no one to help me. He had made me isolate from anyone that cared about me, and he made it seem like any relationship outside of him was disrespectful and for the disrespect I would be punished. He promised to work on himself – even see a therapist – but that didn't last. I was brainwashed, broken, and afraid.

An ex tried to help me by connecting me with some executives he knew to help me get a better paying job. This was all done in secret because "how dare you try to get a better paying job?!" Of course, he found out (he looked for things and reasons to fuss) and then that turned into being accused of cheating with the ex among others. If I stayed late at work, he'd accuse me of lying and cheating. It was impossible to make moves to better myself. He always shut it down.

### 3 - Who did you talk to during the abuse?

I didn't talk to anyone. HUGE MISTAKE. Early in our relationship during the 'what's your favorite color' phase, we had a convo about privacy. I've never been one to be super into social media, and I am mostly private. Not going to post about private things, but I am VERY close with my sister and we talked about everything. Later, when he realized I was telling my sister just about everything, he created tension to isolate me from her. Same with my mom and brother. They are the people I am closest to, but he isolated me from everyone. If I said I was going to meet my mom for dinner, it was an argument and I was accused of cheating or neglecting my marriage. No one was allowed at the house. He'd kick people out if he was the tiniest bit upset. He wouldn't let me have company over. It was an argument every time. He went as far as to accuse me of having a sexual relationship with my brother because I wanted him to stay with me while he was home from college for summer break and Malcolm was at an eight-week work thing in Kansas City. He claimed the neighbors would think something was up if there was another man walking in and out of his house.

So, I didn't talk to anyone. I hid it because I thought all couples had problems, and you shouldn't air your dirty laundry. I didn't know I was being abused and I didn't want to make him angry.

### 4 - Describe the affair in detail and what led you to the arms of another.

The affair was brought on by my need for affection and an

escape from the traumatic relationship I had been experiencing with Malcolm. It was like I was suffocating and suppressing my emotions and the affair provided a brief stent of fresh air. I thought at that moment that the affair was an outlet that was simple and stress free. My affair was the conception of all my suppressed emotions carried out to full term. I talked about this in greater detail in **Chapter 5**.

## 5 - What did you learn about yourself looking back? What would you tell your older and future self?

I was naive. I was manipulated by a narcissistic abuser. It was not my fault and there was nothing I could have done to change the way things happened.

I wish I had opened up to someone and not kept his craziness a secret. Someone could have helped me sooner realize that I was in an abusive relationship. I wish I hadn't listened to my dad about how great of a guy he was. I wish I had the courage to do what I wanted versus doing what I thought I was "supposed" to do.

That is my biggest takeaway…I did what I thought I was supposed to do, and I shouldn't have. I have had to UNLEARN that part of me and learn to be true to myself. There has been a lot of UNLEARNING.

## 6- When you left the house for good, what were you thinking, feeling, hearing, smelling? What time of day or night? What was in your hands? Recap this.

It wasn't the first time I tried to leave. I had talked to myself about it. He had kicked me out and I actually walked out before. This was just the time I had the strength and means to stay gone.

It was Sunday, September 7, 2015. Labor Day weekend. We decided to rewatch the Star Wars saga, episodes one to six in order.

So, we were on the couch watching Star Wars. Something in the movie triggered him. I have no clue what it was. A strong breeze could blow outside, and he'd get mad and start coming at my neck. So, something in the movie triggers him and he starts with the interrogation. That's what I called it. He'd go at it for hours asking questions to get me caught up to find something else to get mad about to make me more confused. Well, he gets mad and goes into the "You're selfish, evil, no one would want you" and I just couldn't take it anymore. STAR WARS had set him off. I mean come on, really?! I KNEW I hadn't done anything to deserve it this time, and I knew this was going to be my life, and I just couldn't do it anymore. Mid-sentence, I stood up (his sentence of course because I never got to talk) and went through the kitchen towards the door and the bathroom was down there too. He probably thought I was going to the bathroom which is why he didn't get up. But I grabbed my purse and keys and went straight to my car.

I don't think I said anything at all. There was nothing to be said. I had on sweatpants and an oversized tee. I already had a packed bag in my car. I had been moving things piece by piece for weeks. It was late morning, noonish. Once I was in the car, I immediately started crying. I called my mom and said, "I left. I'm coming to you." She had no idea what was going on. Once I got out of the neighborhood, I pulled off somewhere to compose myself. I remember thinking you can't cry and drive. I had to make sure he hadn't followed me. He had chased me in his car before, cutting me off, blowing the horn, tailgating…but he hadn't this time. I think I cried the entire day. He called and called and called and called and called. Back to back, hang up and call again. In between the calls, he would text. He was making threats with more name calling. I blocked him at some point so the calls would stop. He called from a blocked number, left angry voicemails, then he switched to email.

I remember this day because I wanted a restraining order. My mother and I went by her house to file for one. They were out of jurisdiction and no help. It was also a Sunday and the next station said the person that did that was out for the weekend. Meanwhile, he's still calling and texting NONSTOP. The next day was Monday, LABOR DAY. The police station in the city we were in couldn't process anything because courts were closed due to the holiday. It was a wet day, and my mom and I were wandering around the courthouse and police station trying to get a protective order with NO LUCK. His mom started calling me. In tears, I told her where I was and that my next step was to report him to his supervision officer for abuse. She relayed the message to him, and the tone changed. More "I'm sorry" and "Please come back so when can talk about it."

## 7 - Where are you now or headed in your life?

Romantically, I am engaged to my soulmate! After years of more bad relationships and much more healing, we found each other. I relocated to my hometown and we now live together.

Professionally, I quit my corporate job to come back home. I am now a full-time entrepreneur. I am much happier even though business is entirely new to me and not what I was groomed for. Remember the 'supposed to's.'

## 8 - What's your mission and why?

My mission is to live in my own truth, to do what makes ME happy in spite of what all the outside influences say. I want to know me. I believe I am a beautiful person and I want to show her to the world as is. I am committed to personal growth and breaking down the societal stigmas that tend to hold women back.

## 9 - What would you say to your abuser?

He kept in touch with me up until about December of 2019. He used to reach out just to ask about my family. I'd be cordial. The last time he reached out, I told him I was engaged and didn't want to hear from him again. He has honored that so far.

I don't know if I'd ever be okay with a sit-down convo with him. Seems weird, but I would say to him that I've healed and moved on. He is a narcissist and I know that no matter what I said, he'd find a way to still blame me.

I'll think about this some more, I never really thought deep into it.

## What would you say to a woman that may find themselves in your situation?

Do NOT KEEP IT A SECRET! Talk about it, listen to those who he cuts you off from. You deserve so much better than this and it's not the end for you. You can escape and be better.

## 10 - What do you know about abuse?

I have learned so much since we split. He was a narcissist, authoritarian personality. I also fell into a stereotype of being young, naive, and eager to make it work. It was actually very surreal when I was learning. Everything I read was exactly what happened to me. I thought I was alone, so it was comforting that I wasn't the only woman to be bamboozled by an abuser.

## 11 - What do you want the reader to take away from each chapter and the entirety of the book?

I just wish I had had help. I was isolated so I didn't know what was happening. I'd like the reader to see the signs to KNOW that they are in an abusive relationship. That knowledge in itself changes things. From the book, I don't want pity. I made the decision I made, and I have lived with it. That relationship forced me to discover Brittany, the woman. I would like people to see that they are not a victim of circumstance. You do have power and control. You are special and loved.

You, beloved, on the flip side of this book. To tell you the truth, this was written with you in mind. Your truth deserves an audience regardless of the pain. The true story locked on the inside has a key. Use your voice as the key. It is the tool that frees you from your past.

Ask me how I know. To be honest, I wrote this book scared and with many conflicting thoughts. Telling my truth about my battle with abuse isn't just contained within these pages, it is forever branded in my heart and mind. I said to myself over and over that I wasn't ready, but it's time. Now I say to you, it's your time. It is your turn to break the shackles of the abuse. No matter the form it showed up in your life, it has to go. Tell the truth scared or not scared! Tell the truth free or bound! The truth must be told while you are alive because I've given you a lifeline.

# REFLECTIONS

**(Feel free to journal your thoughts and learning experiences by answering the questions below)**

HOW DID YOU FEEL WHEN READING THIS CHAPTER?

_____

_____

_____

_____

_____

WHAT DID YOU LEARN?

_____

_____

_____

_____

_____

HOW CAN YOU USE THIS INFORMATION TO HELP SOMEONE ELSE IN LIFE?

_____

_____

_____

_____

_____

HOW DOES THE CONTENT OF THIS CHAPTER RELATE TO YOUR LIFE EXPERIENCE(S)?

_____

_____

_____

_____

_____

# BIBLIOGRAPHY

National Domestic Violence Hotline:

**https://www.thehotline.org/resources/statistics/**

**RESOURCES**

**The National Domestic Violence Hotline**

- Call 800-799-SAFE (7233).

- Staff is available 24 hours a day, 7 days a week.

- Get information in more than 170 languages.

- You will hear a recording and may have to wait for a short time.

- Hotline staff offer safety planning and crisis help. They can connect you to shelters and services in your area.

- Staff can send out written information on topics such as domestic violence, sexual assault, and the legal system.

- You can also get help through email or live chat on the hotline's contact page (link is external).

## The National Dating Abuse Helpline

- Call 866-331-9474 or 866-331-8453 (TDD).

- Staff is available 24 hours a day, 7 days a week.

- You will hear a recording and may have to wait for a short time.

- You can get help through a live online chat from 5 p.m. to 3 a.m. ET. Learn more about the National Dating Abuse Helpline live chat (link is external).

- You can also chat with helpline staff via email or text "loveis" to 22522.

## The National Sexual Assault Hotline

- Call 800-656-4673.

- Staff is available 24 hours a day, 7 days a week.

- You will hear a recording that asks whether you prefer English or Spanish and whether you want to talk to a hotline staff member.

- You can get live online help through the National Sexual Assault Online Hotline (link is external) in English or Spanish.

# ABOUT THE AUTHOR

Brittany Foster Hall is a native of Virginia Beach, VA. She attended Norfolk State University to obtain her B.S. in Biology and continued on to receive her Master's in Public Health and Epidemiology from Eastern Virginia Medical School in 2013. Throughout all her educational and professional accomplishments, she suffered at the hand of an abusive husband. The abuse she suffered has motivated her to not only heal from the trauma and find her own happiness, but to share that knowledge and empower other women who find themselves in similar circumstances. She is now a business owner, motivational speaker, and life coach with the mission to eliminate the stigmas surrounding domestic violence victims and uplift her sisters in their own journeys to confidence and peace.

Made in the USA
Columbia, SC
12 January 2022

54158507R00061